BFI FILM CLASSICS

Edward Buscombe
SERIES EDITOR

Colin MacCabe and David Meeker
SERIES CONSULTANTS

Cinema is a fragile medium. Many ~~~~~~~~~~~~~~~~~ the past now exist, if at all, in damaged or inc ~~~~~~~~. Concerned about the deterioration in the physical state of our film heritage, the National Film and Television Archive, a Division of the British Film Institute, has compiled a list of 360 key films in the history of the cinema. The long-term goal of the Archive is to build a collection of perfect showprints of these films, which will then be screened regularly at the Museum of the Moving Image in London in a year-round repertory.

BFI Film Classics is a series of books commissioned to stand alongside these titles. Authors, including film critics and scholars, film-makers, novelists, historians and those distinguished in the arts, have been invited to write on a film of their choice, drawn from the Archive's list. Each volume presents the author's own insights into the chosen film, together with a brief production history and a detailed filmography, notes and bibliography. The numerous illustrations have been specially made from the Archive's own prints.

With new titles published each year, the BFI Film Classics series will rapidly grow into an authoritative and highly readable guide to the great films of world cinema.

Could scarcely be improved upon ... informative, intelligent, jargon-free companions.
The Observer

Cannily but elegantly packaged BFI Classics will make for a neat addition to the most discerning shelves.
New Statesman & Society

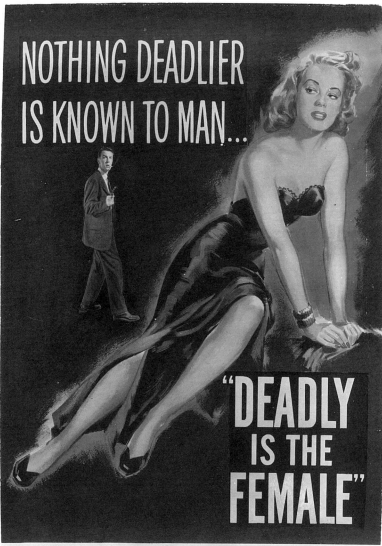

Poster for the first release, under the original title

BFI FILM

CLASSICS

GUN CRAZY

· · · · · · · · · · · · · · · · · ·

Jim Kitses

BRITISH FILM INSTITUTE

bfi

BFI PUBLISHING

First published in 1996 by the
BRITISH FILM INSTITUTE
21 Stephen Street, London W1P 2LN

The British Film Institute exists
to promote appreciation, enjoyment, protection and
development of moving image culture in and throughout the
whole of the United Kingdom.
Its activities include the National Film and
Television Archive; the National Film Theatre;
the Museum of the Moving Image;
the London Film Festival; the production and
distribution of film and video; funding and support for
regional activities; Library and Information Services;
Stills, Posters and Designs; Research;
Publishing and Education; and the monthly
Sight and Sound magazine.

British Library Cataloguing-in-Publication Data
A catalogue record for this book is available from the British Library

ISBN 0–85170–579–0

Stills courtesy of United Artists

Designed by
Andrew Barron & Collis Clements Associates

Typesetting by
D R Bungay Associates, Burghfield, Berks.

Printed in Great Britain by
The Trinity Press, Worcester

CONTENTS

. . . .

For John Kitses
M/Sgts. Ed Leilus and Aaron Freeman
Dr William Burto
Paddy Whannel
and
Alex Jacobs . . . straight-shooters all

ACKNOWLEDGMENTS

Thanks to Ed Buscombe for his enthusiasm, support and patience. My warmest gratitude to John Fell and Scott Simmon for their kind and valuable responses to an early and overlong draft, and to Margo Kasdan, Gregg Rickman and, again, ever-helpful Scott Simmon for close readings of the final manuscript. Gillian Hartnoll was as gracious as ever in making available the services of the BFI Library, and I am indebted to David Meeker for helping me track down Peggy Cummins at the very last minute. The staffs of the Academy Library of Motion Picture Arts and Sciences (Beverly Hills, CA), The Film Center, School of the Art Institute of Chicago, and the Kendall Young Library (Webster City, Iowa), all provided valuable assistance. For help with stills I am beholden to Peggy Cummins, Jack Shadoian, Mitzi Trumbo, and Ann Wilkins of the Wisconsin Center for Film and Theatre Research.

In researching this study I had occasion to speak to many scholars of film noir and Joseph H. Lewis, and I thank them all; however, I must single out William K. Everson, Tim Hunter, Paul Schrader, and Alain Silver, all of whom were especially accommodating. I owe a special debt to Peggy Cummins and Derek Dunnett for warmly welcoming me into their home and sharing their memories. My thanks as well to Joseph H. Lewis for his chats with me, and to Tim Kantor, Millard Kaufman, Arthur Penn and Christopher Trumbo for their kind responses to my queries.

Criticism draws its blood from the teaching situation; I would be remiss indeed if I did not acknowledge all the students who have contributed to this study. I hope that many of them see this book and enjoy it. My appreciation goes as well to my supportive colleagues in the College of Creative Arts and its outstanding Cinema Department at San Francisco State University for a semester's leave which greatly facilitated the writing.

I am grateful to Christopher Williams, Stephanie McKnight, and Clementine for making London visits so pleasant, to Barry Brann for his inimitable L.A. hospitality, and to Margo Kasdan and Gary Kluge for the timely loan of Whispering Pines. Finally, a special thank you and love to Paula for providing spirit, space and encouragement, and to Angela, Jesse and Anastasia, for their inspiration.

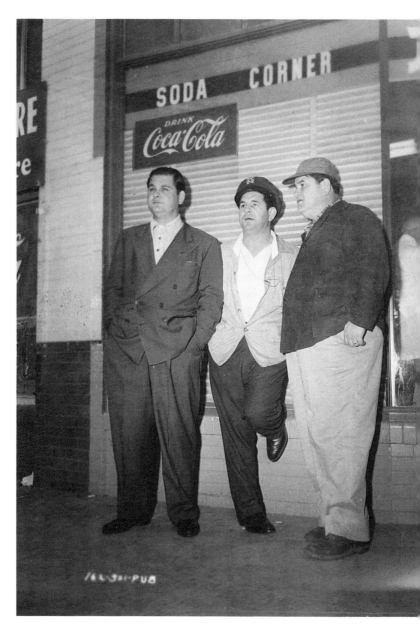

The King Brothers on location with *Gun Crazy*: (r. to l.) Frank, Maurice and Herman King

1
....

If ever a film opened with a defining moment in a young character's life, that film is *Gun Crazy*. A peak achievement of film noir, the dark crime and failure stories that dominate the post-war American cinema, *Gun Crazy* plunges its audience into the shadows from its very first shot. In a bad dream that rapidly becomes nightmare, a dark and private desire is indulged and retribution is instantaneous. This is your life, Bart Tare.

Gun Crazy opens *in medias res* and *in medias noir*, in the middle, that is, of Bart Tare's attempted theft of a gun, and in the midst of a veritable cloudburst of classical noir image coding. In a brilliant little expressionist poem, a tableau comprising some nine shots and seventy seconds, *Gun Crazy* presents us with the fundamentals of the noir formula: a deviant act in a dark and oppressive world, an isolated, alienated and obsessed hero, temptation, failure and defeat. There is a theatrical flavour to it all, a bravura distillation of the essentials, an exemplary vignette captured on stage and in frame in a series of snapshots: a dark, rainy street; a boy, standing, staring at us; the boy framed by and looking in the window; the boy's face, possessed, fascinated, looking; a display of handguns, the centrepiece an ivory-handled Western-style six-shooter; the face receding, a neon sign pulsing behind on–off, on–off; the boy winding up and pitching his rock; the boy posed crucified against the broken window; the sheriff's face, huge and hard; the sprawled boy's look up, a world of wet.

More than a dream, it is a feverish masturbatory fantasy, the furtive hand reaching through the broken glass, the boy trying to get off with his gun, the wetness and the fall, the castrating gaze of the Father and the Law. Introducing the film's basic strategy, the violent is here coloured with the erotic, a conceit enhanced by the long-take shot which builds from the opening credit on, the slow, focused intensity coming to a violent climax, almost comical in its explosive release of tension. We are left with Bart as the butt of the noir universe's joke, the teenager as fall guy, the pathetic loser.

In a stylistic flip-flop somewhat reminiscent of *Citizen Kane*'s famous opening, which fades from the dark inner recesses of Kane's extinguishing consciousness to the bright 'objective' world of the 'News on the March' account of his life and career, *Gun Crazy* dissolves from Bart lying in the gutter of his defeated dream to the sun-drenched courtroom of evidence and testimony, law and justice, that seeks to make sense of the boy and his actions. It may seem outrageous to mention *Kane* in the same breath as our little epic; however, parallels do come to mind. The courtroom scene, for instance, will proceed through the testimony of Ruby, Bart's sister, his friends, and his teacher, each resulting in a flashback (the opening scene logically the sheriff's) as in the main narrative of *Kane*, as the judge tries to get to the bottom of Bart's obsession with *his* Rosebud – guns.

During this testimony, the *mise-en-scène* stresses Bart's impotence, supplying us visually with a set of variations on a still life – a hangdog Bart immobile in a chair – in place of the opening's images of Bart in mesmerised action. The climax of that scene is of course the boy's pitching of the rock at the window through which we view him, an attempt to break into the store, but also a futile attempt to break out, and to reach out, of his constraining world. For Bart freedom evidently resides with the gun, and for his dangerous act of breaking the glass, the law, and very nearly the illusionist distance between audience and spectacle, the boy is banished in the ensuing scene to the far corners of the frame, a series of deep focus compositions holding him to one side and against a courtroom window, a safe distance from the site of testimony in the foreground. Again, the visual design may recall *Kane* and the image of the young Charlie playing in the snowy distance ('The Union forever'), trapped within the dark window frame before which his fate is being sealed.

In drawing these parallels to the American cinema's most famous and influential work, I am not trying to borrow prestige, or to blur the radical differences that exist. *Gun Crazy*'s stunning achievement is intimately bound up with, and a direct result of, its relatively low-budget, low-class origins. Its genealogy is distinctly minor league; *Gun Crazy* is at the opposite end of the spectrum from *Citizen Kane* in terms of production values, authorial stature and power, historical significance. Humble Bart Tare is destined to become neither capitalist titan nor cultural icon. Instead of an American colossus, citizen Tare will be very much the typical noir protagonist – an unknown soldier, a small-time guy. But for all its modesty of subject and means, the film does resemble its heavyweight predecessor in some crucial respects; stylistically, it is an extraordinarily inventive work, and it too lays claim to our attention as one of those films that is quintessentially *American*.

2

....

Gun Crazy's inspired, lurid title hurtles on to the screen with the tabloid pizzazz of a headline. Just to complicate matters, however, *Gun Crazy* was originally released by United Artists in January 1950 as *Deadly is the Female*, then re-released six months later under the title of the source material, MacKinlay Kantor's *Saturday Evening Post* short story. Such a spin was clearly possible on a narrative summarised by the office of Motion Picture Production Code chief Joseph Breen, the guardian of the era's morality whose authorial interventions in the script's development had been extensive, as: 'a man's mania for guns is capitalised upon by an adventuress . . . and both lose their lives after a career of crime.'[1]

If the different titles problematised the question of whether Bart or his sharp-shooting inamorata, Laurie, owned the narrative and was responsible for its violence, the ill-advised attempt to avoid exploitational overtones with poetic inversion failed to fool a discerning *Variety*: 'Hiding behind the awkward title . . . is a story of desperate young love and crime.'[2] In any case, the film was well received by a savvy local and trade press, the sharp critic in the *Los Angeles Times* impressed that 'a crime picture can come along at this late date and top nearly all that have preceded it . . . hell on wheels . . . use of the medium in its sharpest, simplest sense.'[3]

Where a sophisticated eye saw iconographic purity, the more jaded view of national reviewers was dismissive – 'humdrum pulp fiction'.[4] Although inevitably hurt by its uncertain release, it is doubtful whether the film could have done well in any case. What did it have going for it? No powerful imperialist studio logo roared a promise of prestige or glamour at the audience. MGM reportedly wanted to buy the film and lend their marketing clout, but a condition was the removal of the King Brothers' producers credit, in studio eyes synonymous with cheapjack product. The feisty Kings – the 'B-picture Kings', Frank, Maurie and Hymie – predictably refused. *Gun Crazy* was doomed to become one of the great cult movies of American film history, the favourite B-movie of everybody-in-the-know. But what everybody would not know is that the film was conceived and released as a modest A-level production. The romantic myth surrounding the film has it the achievement of an auteur inspired by shoestring limitations to create the very epitome of B-film noir. Ironically, the truth is that the enterprising Kings – Monogram

Studio masters of the cheapie and quickie, of formula efforts with no stars and lean budgets – were attempting to upgrade with *Gun Crazy*, and its proposed $500,000 budget and thirty-day schedule, to come in at the floor of the A-level production, the so-called 'nervous A'. Yet the film must have screamed 'B-movie!' at its original audiences, as it has at their successors.[5]

One can see why. Despite aiming high (for them), the Kings were inevitably to live down to their reputation somewhat in mounting the production. The economising would be obvious in the small scale, the few crowd scenes, the stock footage. To helm the project they had originally considered art director Gordon Wiles, whom they had direct *The Gangster* the previous year, but in the end they brought in Joseph H. Lewis, a veteran of successful B-movie and, more recently, 'nervous A' studio assignments. But the crucial factor was the casting. The Kings had originally gone after both Gregory Peck and Dana Andrews for Bart, and later there was talk of pairing the likes of Farley Granger and Susan Hayward to play the outlaw couple. However, in the eyes of Hollywood's elite, lowbrow Monogram and the proletarian Kings were a standing joke, sources of the worst pictures on the market. Moreover, *Gun Crazy* was going into production while the jury was still out on more ambitious independent projects. Established stars were understandably wary of leaving big studio lots to share in the poorboy Kings' gamble – capitalising on the success of small pictures such as their earlier *When Strangers Marry* and *Dillinger* to try to move up. Ultimately, the Kings were forced to go with minor stars John Dall and Peggy Cummins, both a B-minus in name voltage, casting which would result in full-blooded and sensitive performances, but which lacked iconographic oomph.

In short, *Gun Crazy* both benefited and suffered from changes in the industrial landscape, as did its director. As Paul Kerr has argued, economic developments in Hollywood such as the break-up of block booking attendant on the Supreme Court anti-trust rulings in 1946–8, and the consequent divestiture of the studios' exhibition arm, boosted the efforts of enterprising independents like the Kings, and were critical factors in shaping the contours of film noir and the careers of B-movie directors such as Lewis.[6] A system in flux was opening up new directions for creative work, as evidenced by the limited but real advance in resources for a minuscule B-movie such as Columbia's *My Name is Julia Ross* (1945). A 65-minute thriller with Nina Foch as the put-upon

heroine, this modest picture was recognised as a sleeper by studio head
Harry Cohn while it was in production, and given more shooting time,
a preview and an independent release. It was a breakthrough for director
Lewis, whose career so far had consisted of some two dozen quickies at
various studios – mostly Western and action movies on which Lewis
would often leave his idiosyncratic touch, long, long takes and deep-
focus shots framed by wagon-wheels or such in the foreground.

But it was *Gun Crazy* that was to provide Lewis's only real breakthrough: a tight, evocative script, the support of independent-minded

(l. to r.) Producer Frank King and cinematographer Russell Harlan, standing;
Peggy Cummins and director Joseph H. Lewis, seated above

street-fighter producers, performances by two gifted, offbeat players, censors' interventions on behalf of a pushy *Zeitgeist* – all coming together with his stylish, inventive direction in a remarkable synergy. The result was a *bona fide* American masterpiece, pint-sized though it may be, one of Hollywood's transcendent works, an indispensable portrait of a transitional moment and ethos, a world of small-time characters and big-time aspirations, brought to life in a genuine desert island movie (if the ship is sinking . . .). Starting in the late 1960s, auteur critics made valiant efforts to attribute the authorship of *Gun Crazy* to Lewis. In vain. A hodgepodge of a filmography absolutely resists reduction to any consistency, and provides vivid evidence of how dependent Lewis always was on collaborators. Although there are a number of interesting films, especially the distinguished, Philip Yordan-scripted, upper-echelon noir, *The Big Combo* (1955), as an auteur Lewis is essentially a stylist without a theme, and it is *Gun Crazy* that provides his body of work with its centre of gravity.

But it was not so much auteurism that drew the film into the spotlight in the 60s as the spectacular success of what some thought to be a direct descendant, the Arthur Penn-directed *Bonnie and Clyde*. Perhaps it was the visual link of the beret that both heroines sport, after the most famous photograph of the original Bonnie, but many critics invoked *Gun Crazy*, and in some cases preferred it. Over the years *Gun Crazy* has received a goodly share of attention for its pivotal place in the distinguished company of the fugitive-couple narrative cycle. Where Fritz Lang's depression-era *You Only Live Once* and Nicholas Ray's *They Live By Night* (1948) see their subjects as innocent victims, the King Brothers were clearly more interested in the greater commercial potential gained by centring the romantic narrative on rebellious characters who actively choose to be criminals, as is suggested by press stories released during shooting which focused on Cummins as a 'female Dillinger'.[7] And it is of course this radical shift in moral weight that gives the film its hard edge, and thereafter informs *Bonnie and Clyde* and its own offspring, *Badlands*, as well as the latter-day post-modern efforts, *True Romance* and *Natural Born Killers*. That our small picture continues to exert its specific influence is also evident in Tamra Davis's homage, *Guncrazy* – wherein the seed idea of an uncontrollable fascination with guns is recycled – as well as in its mark on such distinguished neo-noir as *Blue Steel* and *Red Rock West*.

If the film's subversive focus and energy were overlooked at the time in America and Britain, this was due in part to the absence of critical methods and cultural perspectives. In France the Surrealist Ado Kyrou seized on *Gun Crazy* in his *Le Surréalisme au cinéma* (1953) as 'an admirable film, which alone of all cinema clearly marks the road which leads from *l'amour fou* to *la révolte folle*.'[8] To the Surrealists the film appealed as a celebration of exalted, delirious love leading to the social rebellion of its characters, the couple in these terms seen, charmingly, as spiritual kin to Buñuel's scandalous lovers at the outset of *L'Age d'or*, rolling in the mud, locked in sexual embrace.

As Jack Shadoian has demonstrated, *Gun Crazy* can sustain such a reading: doomed by their passion, the couple are like 'wild animals' whom society must drive off its paved roads into a wild-nature preserve where it will hound the pair to their deaths.[9] But in my view the couple are less singular rebels, wolves outside civilisation's circle, than prototypes of the lapsed citizenry of film noir, American heretics, fugitives from the work ethic and throwbacks to a rough-and-ready Manifest Destiny. Building on the Surrealist line, Raymonde Borde and Etienne Chaumeton in their ground-breaking study *Panorama du film noir américain* (1955) crowned the film as 'a kind of Golden Age of American film noir', their study establishing the beguiling poetic label that has both sustained and frustrated generations of critics and scholars since with its amorphousness.[10] And it is as a defining noir text, a landmark on the artistic map which film noir provides to the social and emotional topography of post-war America, capitalism and American populist ideology, that *Gun Crazy* in my view most repays attention.

3

. . . .

If study of the film's production history and personnel discourages simple attribution of authorship to its director, the thought of *Gun Crazy* without Lewis is unthinkable. Dominating the film, his taut visual strategies invariably orchestrate the action in terms of maximum economy and expressiveness, capping the cumulative process of streamlining that had begun with censors' suggestions and evolved through successive script drafts. A case in point, the opening displays a typically unerring instinct for camera placement which delivers complex meanings with an elegantly functional *mise-en-scène*. As is often the case in the film, the coverage of the action is organised here around one shot, the perspective from inside the store window interrupted only by insert close-ups of boy and gun to underline the obsessional force of the rain, the dark window frame, the shadow of the guns, the haunted stare. The result is an extreme compression and simplicity of visual logic that invite a Zen-like con-templation of the events depicted. The boy is introduced 'under the gun' of a hostile world, the rain descending through the darkness like laser bullets, and is then defined by the guns in the window, the framing trapping him until he breaks free only to find himself locked into the authority of the law. The effect is close to what one suspects Alexandre Astruc had in mind in the heyday of the *nouvelle vague* when he advanced his theory of *la caméra-stylo*, of a kind of pure writing with the camera.

And what is written here is a virtual primer on film noir, and especially classical noir codes. 'A dark street in the early morning hours, splashed with a sudden downpour. Lamps form haloes in the murk.'[11] Thus Higham and Greenberg's *Hollywood in the Forties*, as they attempt to define 'the specific ambience of film noir'. Apropos this kind of setting, Paul Schrader suggested that 'there seems to be an almost Freudian attachment to water. . . . the rainfall tends to increase in direct proportion to the drama'.[12]

To read these standard accounts of noir, one would think that the rain it raineth every day in these actually quite diverse movies. Like fog and mist, rain is symbolic weather that represents an intensification of noir's darkness (its 'murk'), the shadow-world rendered spatially as not only mysterious and dangerous, but destabilising, turbulent, hostile. Thus these climatic disturbances often occur at key moments, turning points in the action, underlining a character's loss of control or fateful change of direction. So it is that we have the pathetic hero of *Detour* facing disaster in a driving rainstorm, Walter in *Double Indemnity* watching Phyllis leave in the rainy night, realising that 'the machinery had started to move and nothing could stop it'.

Arguably, however, the most imaginative use of this coding comes nearly ten years after *Double Indemnity* helped to establish the vogue for this new kind of downbeat crime film, and comes not in a noir at all, but in a musical. *Singin' in the Rain* (1952) aggressively offers itself as a denial of the noir vision of America as a shadow-world of failure, and in

Gene Kelly's solo title song and dance, marshals all of the musical's considerable expressive resources to affirm the vitality of the American dream in the very teeth of the noir climate, to retake the high ground after nearly ten years of noir gloom and doom. 'Come on with the rain, I've a smile on my face.' At one level, the number functions within the narrative as a sublime expression of the state of being in love. But what elevates this number to the status of *the* icon of American popular culture is its celebration and incarnation of quintessential American values, its paean to the common man, its testament to faith in the possibilities of success in the face of adversity. 'I belonged to the sweatshirt generation,' Kelly has said, 'and wanted to make the dance, in costume and move-ment, akin to the world we were living in. I wanted to dance like sailors, fighters, steelworkers and truck drivers.'[13] Kelly's democratic image – his can-do, know-how kind of guy – contributes strongly to the sense of American ideology on parade here. The positivist strain of American character has often been remarked on, the belief in America as a special place, a chosen people. Writing in 1835, the French visitor Gustave de Beaumont observed:

> . . . the American remains unshaken by any misfortune. The most unexpected blow, the most imminent peril, find him impassive. Strange contrast! He pursues fortune with extreme ardor, and calmly bears all adversity. Nothing stops him in his undertakings; nothing discourages his efforts; when faced by an obstacle, no matter how great, he will never say 'I cannot'. Bold, patient, indefatigable, he tries again. This people is steadfastly faithful to its origins; for it was born of exiles, and men who will travel 3,000 miles across the sea in search of a new fatherland must have a fund of energy in their souls.[14]

The joy of dance that Kelly expresses, the openness and charm, freedom and mobility, energy and confidence, are overwhelming. As Paddy Whannel would point out with reference to the achievement of the MGM musical in sequences such as Kelly's here, or the bandstand number graced by Bob Fosse and Betty Garrett in *My Sister Eileen*, what is created is not a spirit that separates the audience from performer and spectacle in its awe at unattainable skills, but rather a contagious populist flavour, an inspiring invitation to the dance.[15] All the coded elements that are employed poetically to trip, trap and defeat Bart Tare (and hundreds of other noir characters) are here answered, resisted and disarmed. The mystification and oppression of the rainy night with its darkness and shadows, the desolation of the city setting of empty street and closed shops, the lateness of the hour, the threat of the police and the stranger – all these icons of fear and paranoia become the site and props for this dynamic display of American spirit and style. The exuberant triumph of this moment may be seen to flow in part from its rising above – as Kelly does, literally, with his soaring leap up to the lamp-post – the dispirited and often downtrodden image of the average American that is at the centre of so many noir works. As Robert Warshow pointed out in his ground breaking study of the gangster film, the persistent and pervasive emphasis in America on success and the individual inevitably creates a compensating ideological structure in the narrative trajectory of the classic gangster's rise and fall, wherein failure is played out, allowed, and thus validated.[16] In many ways film noir also plays this role and continues this process, its narratives failure stories set in a shadow-world, a dark landscape that parallels and critiques official America.

4

. . . .

Gun Crazy's own rainy street scene features Rusty Tamblyn as Bart Tare at fourteen. Although no Kelly, Tamblyn was to go on (as Russ) to his own small success as an actor/dancer in musicals, most visibly *Seven Brides for Seven Brothers* and *West Side Story*. Fair, freckled and innocent, Tamblyn is kin to what might be called the Mark Twain prototype, and his presence in the early scenes of *Gun Crazy* helps to introduce an iconography, typing and behaviour that consistently evokes mainstream America as a theme.

The chronology of *Gun Crazy* suggests it is the late 30s as the film opens – Bart will spend four years in reform school, perhaps another four in the army, to emerge after the war. However, the rural small town setting and the Western milieu suggest a community in touch with a much earlier America, a world still informed by nineteenth-century frontier styles and mores. Thus the opening scene's spatial lay-out and architecture are evocative of the classic Western town; and the prominent feed and grain sign on the left, and the rifles in the store window frame-right, provide strong balancing accents between which Bart is positioned. This atmosphere is forcefully underlined by the close-up on the six-shooter that Bart evidently craves, and the unmistakable iconographic impact of the sheriff with his Stetson, moustache and star, played by Trevor Bardette, a veteran Western performer. The transitional flavour of this historical moment is nicely captured in the hardware store display, evidently an expression of regional pride and a memento of a past era when such weaponry was common in frontier life. However, the assumption that the six-shooter – and the violent world it represents – is now part of distant American history, and can be safely placed on show in store windows, is here revealed to be as fragile as the glass shattered by Bart's rock.

The rural flavour persists in the courtroom, where Bart's trial is an informal affair conducted on a first-name basis. At first glance the proceedings seem unthreatening, the community supportive, Bart even represented by two solemn little friends, Dave and Clyde, as character witnesses. Bart loves guns, but it is established that he is not driven by the politics of 'production for use', the economic theory which Hildy, in *His*

Rusty Tamblyn as the young Bart

Girl Friday, introduces as a possible source of the urge to fire that has put Earl Williams into a death-cell. Nonetheless, society must be regulated and its property and institutions protected. Treating Bart rather like a dangerous virus, Morris Carnovsky, the small-town Solomon presiding, banishes the boy rather than risk giving him into the care of his sister and her fiancé: 'Adjusting yourself to marriage, Ruby, is a job all by itself, without assuming extra handicaps at the start.'

What is Bart's problem? Why his 'dangerous mania' for guns? The film invites the speculation that a needy, fatherless boy may have fixed on guns in his yearning for self-definition and manhood, the story of Bart's life one of a structuring absence. If this 'dollar-book Freud' – Welles's term for Rosebud – is not explored in the film, its presence is unmistakable in MacKinlay Kantor's original story, and his screenplay adaptation which expanded on it. Two aspects of the story stand out. Laurie's prototype, Antoinette ('Toni') McReady, briefly appears in the carnival shooting contest, serving as catalyst in Bart's graduation to serious crime, but promptly disappears when they are imprisoned after their second job; so the story is Bart's. Equally significant is the fact that his progress from childhood to notoriety as a 'modern Jesse James' and FBI-designated 'Public Enemy' status is narrated by Dave, the town newspaper editor's son; so the story is Dave's, too.

The desire expressed by Kantor, poet of rustic Americana, was to make an authentic Mid-western picture, and a serious study of delinquency. Kantor's work often consisted of vignettes of American regional and village life based on his own experience; *Gun Crazy* appears to have been an especially personal work. Kantor himself had been a convert from gun enthusiast as a youth to naturalist, and had also grown up fatherless, the elder

Kantor leaving home to achieve notoriety as a confidence man and convict. Like father, like son? Kantor had flirted with a rough crowd as a teenager but had been rescued by his mother, who put him to work assisting her in editing their home town newspaper. At one level, then, the narration by Dave of Bart's story can be seen as a communion between two poles of Kantor's early life, and as the exploration of a shadow Kantor.

Expanding the story for the screen, Kantor explicitly identified the gun craziness of his hero with the themes of the absent father and the Western myth. His script opens with a pre-credit sound montage of gunfire escalating from BB shot through rifle and revolver to machine-gun, as we see the target of a gaudy tin replica of a modern rodeo cowboy progressively blasted away. The credits were to appear over a close-up of a hand curled around 'a .45 Colt, Frontier Model', the gun belonging to Bart's father, Jay Coulter, a World War I veteran who went bad as a result of 'imagining he was Jesse James', and is shot down by a posse in

(l. to r.) Lester Cole, Bette Davis, Dalton Trumbo, Alvah Bessie, daughter Nikola, Albert Maltz, son Christopher, wife Cleo, Frances and Ring Lardner, attorney Ben Margolis, Herbert Biberman

the opening scene. Kantor was suggesting that on the psychological level his young hero's lack was that of a model of masculine identity and moral code associated with the father. However, Kantor was also interested in sustaining an allegorical level of action, suggesting an America wherein violence is inspired and authorised by a dangerous Western myth and ideology that fills the void.

The repressed back story of a heroic outlaw killer of a father throws light on Bart's double bind of love for guns on the one hand, and his inability to pull the trigger on the other, the intolerable dilemma of wanting to be a man like his father and yet to be a man unlike his father. This insight confirms in us what we sense in the film, the confusion in Bart over the direction in which true manhood lies. Bart is not simply a weak character under the thumb of a dominating woman, but is genuinely caught in a conflict between a life of social regulation and the individual ego's unconstrained satisfaction of need and desire; at its most extreme, between the life of law and outlaw.

None of this explicit genealogy survived Dalton Trumbo's scissors. Although Millard Kaufman is credited as the script's co-author, he was fronting for the blacklisted Trumbo, who with *Gun Crazy* began an undercover career spanning some forty-five black market properties. Approached by the enterprising Kings shortly after the Washington House Un-American Activities Committee hearings in the autumn of 1947, Trumbo readily agreed to a rewrite deal for a modest $3,750 to be paid over a year and a half. Appropriately, Trumbo had speed and bucks on his mind – he had bills to pay, promises to keep, and miles to go before he went to prison in June 1950, for contempt of Congress.[17]

Kantor and Trumbo – Mac and Doc – were joined together in a strange, invisible partnership. In some ways they were opposites: Kantor the Mid-western conservative who displayed a block-letter poster above his desk – FUCK COMMUNISM; Trumbo the champion of left-wing causes and the most renowned of the Hollywood Ten. Yet in many ways they were more like positive-negative mirror images, both righteous patriots and ambitious artists who had risen from humble origins. Working his way up from the pulps to quality story markets and the novel, Kantor had been commissioned by Sam Goldwyn to write a piece about returning veterans. Producing *Glory for Me*, the big-name writer had thereafter broken with the mogul, bitter at the absence of any glory for him as source of Robert Sherwood's Oscar-winning script in the studio's publicity for *The Best Years of Our Lives*. Trumbo, of course, had been Hollywood's highest paid scriptwriter until the HUAC hearings. Both had been reduced to working with the cut-rate Kings, with whom they enjoyed close but turbulent relations. Kantor would sever ties in the autumn of 1947, disappointed that a summer shoot of the film on location in his home town of Webster City, Iowa, had been cancelled.

Hired shortly thereafter, Trumbo would produce for the Kings for years, writing, revising, doctoring, continuously bemoaning his exploited status but appreciating the work. Both would go on to bigger things, Kantor winning the Pulitzer prize in 1955 for his Civil War novel *Andersonville*, Trumbo embarrassing official Hollywood with the Oscar in 1957 for the best story for *The Brave One*, another King Brothers production penned under the *nom de plume* of a King nephew, Robert Rich. Both had experienced alienation from mainstream America, Kantor the half-Jewish son of divorce and a renegade father, Trumbo writing under the shadow of a jail term he was appealing. If Kantor's autobiographical links with the story accounted for its intensity, they were also behind the excessive stretch of a screenplay of 180-plus pages. Trumbo's more detached status, his own fugitive, high-speed state of mind, would generate cuts and streamlining that would eventually trim the script to 116 pages. The professional writer rather than the master of agit-prop, Trumbo lay the foundations for the classical unities and balance of the production.

5

Typical of Trumbo's tightening of Kantor's scenario was his surgery on the original's extensive catalogue, stretching over a third of the script, of Bart's youthful problems. In keeping with the modernist tone characteristic of so much noir narration, Trumbo employed a complex time-structure, seizing on Bart's trial as the framework within which to flashback to defining low-points of his childhood - the trauma of killing a chick when he was seven, his inability to pull the trigger on a mountain lion, being caught with a gun at school – before fast forwarding to the main body of the story. If such a radical approach sheared away a gaggle of incidents and characters (including Bart's large, neglectful family), it also made for a more resonant and focused structure.

A good example is how Bart's reunion with his Cashville buddies takes place cheek-by-jowl with their earlier visit to the mountains, the occasion of the boy's failure to fire on the wild cat. The parallelism painfully underscores Bart's lack of progress, Lewis's typically elegant deep-focus shot foregrounding the exploding beer bottles, Bart still showing off his marksmanship. In contrast, the Cashville boys, if they have not travelled far, have fulfilled their destiny. Clyde has become his dad, the leather-jacketed sheriff and father: 'I guess he'll grow up to be sheriff too.'

Kantor's proposition that the son may be a reproduction of the father is suggestively put here, given the void around Bart. Asked his plans, he is evasive – perhaps he'll get a job demonstrating for Remington – and nervously rises (as he talks of 'settling down'), closing his gun case and with it any further discussion. The suggestion of vagueness comes across nicely in John Dall's performance as the older Bart. An intelligent and distinctive actor, Dall alternated between the stage and film work throughout an all too brief career that ended with his death in 1971, at fifty-two. Bart aside, Dall is remembered for two other roles: as the Welsh coalminer and student in *The Corn is Green* (for which he had won an Oscar nomination for best supporting actor in 1945), and the gay-coded, aristocratic psychopath he had just turned in for Hitchcock's *Rope*. Although there are significant differences of class, nationality and character, all three roles are versions of a dependent, vulnerable person-ality, decisively influenced by a mentor – Bette Davis's inspiring teacher, James Stewart's intellectually arrogant professor, Peggy Cummins's sexy sideshow sharpshooter.

Tall, rangy, raw-boned, Dall has an aw-shucks quality that also contributes to the populist flavour, echoing the classic look of 'the Lincoln prototype', one at home in natural settings. [18] The reunion in the mountains serves to underline Bart's small-town rural background, and to make it the privileged site to which the film will return as the setting for Bart and Laurie's last stand. Wherever he has been the past eight years (and the film is typically mute about this), here are his roots, the scene insists, in the haunts and pursuits of a Huck-and-Tom boyhood. If we are reminded of Jefferson Smith's Boy Rangers, fair enough; icono-graphically and emotionally, Cashville is not that far from Mandrake and Bedford Falls, and Frank Capra's celebration of the beneficent effects of nature and small-town America.

However, Bart has not come back to Cashville to settle. Joining the carnival, Bart reveals himself a drifter, one of film noir's recurrent heroes and a privileged American type. Bart's entry into the post-war job market, such as it is, is simultaneously his entry point into the noir 'life'. Stylistically, noir asserts that once the darkness falls within a character, he may cross the boundary into deviant behaviour practically anywhere: the whole town is in the shadows, so to speak. Nevertheless certain sites beyond the rain-drenched street do tend to recur as signifiers of the frontier between the safe, daylight world and its shadow. Bars are of course a prime example: the Til Two in *Shadow of a Doubt* where Uncle Charlie lectures his niece ('The world is a sty'), or *The Big Heat*'s The Retreat, where Vince and the boys hang out. Nightclubs also frequently serve, the *locus classicus* being the scene in *D.O.A.* in which Edmond O'Brien is poisoned at a San Francisco wharfside club, The Fisherman (site of nets and lures), where the black jazz musicians, performing with hysteria and abandon, are said to drive patrons 'jive crazy'. The intensity and hyperbole of the scene – the huge close-ups of sweaty, transfigured black faces, the agitation of the hopped-up, compulsively drinking crowd ('Give us another blast, Leo'), the rapid cutting and blaring music – privilege the moment, suggesting a crucial threshold, the musicians mythological figures, gatekeepers to a hellish odyssey, the deities of a dark America.

What these venues, like the carnival, share is their function in catering to humanity's hunger for release, its need to escape the everyday, to lose one's self; and it is in seeking this kind of release that noir characters often find themselves embarking on a dark journey. From this point of view, the cinema itself is the noir medium par excellence, and understandably the medium of choice for film-makers like the Surrealist Buñuel – who saw film as the nocturnal voyage into the unconscious – and Hitchcock with his fascination with audience psychology. However, the carnival is also potent in feeding the appetite for pleasure and fantasy, in functioning as a distorted, deviant double of the normal world. And it is, appropriately enough, Bluey-Bluey, the carnival clown with whom Bart shares quarters, who articulates the noir function of the carnival as a grotesque comment on capitalism and the work ethic:

Yes, sir, we got the crookest little carnival layout west of the Mississippi. Why, we've got more ways of making suckers than we got suckers! When we pull out of this burg tomorrow morning the natives will have nothing left but some old collar buttons and some rusty bobby pins.

6

Beyond balloons and belly dancers, the carnival boasts as its biggest spectacle Laurie's incarnation of the Western myth. Here again, the attempt to frame and contain America's violent history for the purposes of entertainment will fail; Laurie's show will soon be on the road, and for real. Bart and Laurie's dressing as cowboys for their first big job can be seen as resonating with a symbolic force far beyond that of a utilitarian disguise. Echoing an earlier era's Wild West shows, the shooting exhibition featuring Annie Laurie Starr foregrounds the Western motif hinted at in Bart's obsession with guns. Kantor had Laurie being introduced as having 'the power which won the West', and had envisaged 'Wanted' posters circulating late in the film which featured carnival publicity stills of the two formally posed in their regalia, hands on weapons. If Trumbo's cuts

trimmed back the emphasis on the myth from full-blown theme to resonant subtext, the references to the Western nevertheless provide the
action with an illuminating and ironic framework.

The myth is nothing if not a patriarchal fantasy of male power, and
its empowering effects for young boys has been one source of its
perennial appeal. At the age of seven, Bart was already on wooden
horseback the day he killed a chick. The boy had practised trick shots
(blowing holes in canteens aloft) and, twirling six-guns, must have
dreamt of heroic deeds. Bart and his mates would have grown up with a
popular culture dominated by the traditional Western whose hero acts
out of moral imperatives, and whose superior marksmanship is an
expression of his ethical code. However, such movie fantasies are to be
left far behind in Bart and Laurie's anachronistic saga. Although life
with Laurie will find Bart playing many roles, one he is not equipped to
play is that of the charismatic leader, the guarantor of law and justice, the
Father. The skills that he and Laurie share, absent of any moral purpose,
are to be his undoing.

Given those skills and his isolated state, the sudden introduction of
the beautiful, sharpshooting Laurie into his life has for Bart the force of an
apparition, a dream come true. With her rapidly firing six-guns shooting
skywards as they precede the Western-garbed performer into the low-
angle shot, her quick forward movement effectively expelling the show's
emcee from the frame, Laurie comes to a standstill with both guns high in
a brightly lit medium close-up, smiling coolly as she sizes up her crowd.
Spotting Bart in a front row – an insert reveals him beginning to lean
forward with a broad smile of appreciation – Laurie raises an eyebrow and
punishes him with a shot aimed and fired head-on. He recoils, Laurie
rewards him with a radiant smile, and Bart and the crowd applaud the trick
use of blanks. In its way the moment is as impressive as 'one of the most
stunning entrances in all of cinema', as Edward Buscombe terms John
Wayne's introduction in *Stagecoach*, where director John Ford moves in
rapidly on a cowpoke, rifle a-twirl.[19] In contrast to Ford's dolly shot that
makes the introduction to the young Wayne an up-close and sensitive one,
Lewis's *mise-en-scène* insists on an aggressive character charging forward
and firing, taking possession of the stage and the frame, the self-reflexive
shot at the audience (we share Bart's point of view) recalling the tag shot
in the earliest Western, Edwin S. Porter's *The Great Train Robbery*, and
immediately announcing to both Bart and the audience the presence of a

performer with a dangerously unpredictable nature. Her charming and spirited debut – like that of *Gun Crazy* itself – can be seen as a fair bid for attention, a triumphant seizing of the stage, however small, by Peggy Cummins, an intelligent and talented actress who had yet to find her niche but whose performance was to be absolutely crucial to the achievement of the film.

As Laurie goes through her act, striking poses and smiling at the crowd, Bart is seen to become increasingly mesmerised by the young, diminutive, professional sharpshooter, her abundant hair framing the pretty face below the cowboy hat, the gunbelt and Western-style pants hugging the trim form. We see Bart again leaning forward intently, Clyde nudging Dave behind. We may here recognise a version of the look of fascination that often strikes the noir hero as he encounters the *femme fatale*. Of course, some *femmes* are more *fatale* than others. If Laurie's entrance can be seen as that of the brazen phallic woman, flaunting her usurping of male role and power, the design and execution of the scene do not suggest that she ensnares Bart. Film noir is not nearly as monolithic as terms such as *femme fatale*, spider woman, phallic woman suggest. In terms of noir's dark myth, the encounter with Laurie

should function structurally as the moment of enchantment, the Queen of Night casting her dark spell. However, this charming scene, for all the fireworks a buoyant and witty divertissement with its wry comic tone, is a far cry from the so-called characteristic moods of noir – claustrophobic, despairing, dark, etc. If anything, the scene can be said to celebrate the union of these two strangers, the poetry of the scene crowning the formation of a couple.

The dance of these two characters commences immediately once Bart comes forward and mounts the stage, the electricity palpable. Laurie circles slowly around and behind him, he slowly approaches, thoughtfully scratching his nose and smiling at her. It is all glances, gestures, body language and movements, testifying to a couple of cool, amused characters, to a reciprocal curiosity and mutual attraction. He grins nervously, continuously, she looks arch, smiles, keeps raising an eyebrow. The competition quickly develops ritualistic and symbolic dimensions that collapse combat and courtship. They match each other in the fanning of a fusillade of shots, then Laurie cuts to the chase, upping the ante, asking whether Bart is game to try 'the crowns'; Bart responds, 'Are *you?*' She warns that she once shot low; he repeats after her, 'So did

I.' The suspense builds slowly, along with our delicious sense of this couple's perfect fit, of parallel destinies, of a convergence. The pattern of alternating and balancing responses continues, each donning the crown of matches which the shooter must ignite with the accuracy of their marksmanship. Each shot resonates, set off by the silence in the tent and the music playing quietly in the fairground outside. Bart is the victor. He unnerves Laurie by winking at her before her first shot; she misses her last. Bart pauses for effect before his last shot, then ignites the match to win decisively. The *mise-en-scène* also favours Bart slightly, foregrounding his point of view both when he is the shooter and the shootee, but overall the strategy is one that choreographs characters, space, camera moves, and performance, to emphasise the ritualistic, rhyming structure, the ceremonial quality of the event.

Although Bart wins, they have both passed the tests of skill and courage, they have the magical prowess of the mythical Robin Hood and William Tell, they have held us and shared the stage. In the process, we sense that a couple has been formed. The lighting of matches and smoking of cigarettes, so pervasive in American movies of the period, in noir take on iconic status as signifiers of passion, appetite and desire – people who smoke too much are frustrated, *Gilda*'s men's room attendant, Uncle Pio, tells the heroine. The guns going off, the igniting matches, clearly work this way in this scene; indeed, much of the charm of the moment derives from our appreciation of the neat conjoining of the violent and the erotic. However, the symbolism of the crowns hints at a bond that transcends the carnal. Late in the film, Bart will acknowledge that it's impossible for them to break up, that they go together, 'maybe like guns and ammunition go together'. Amusingly prosaic, the simile underlines the interdependent functioning of the couple as equal partners, soul mates, a status that the symmetry and radiance of their meeting suggests from the outset. Thus the haloes of light signify the final act in the symbolic marriage of two uniquely like-minded individuals, a union marked by the exchange of Laurie's ring, the witnessing of Dave and Clyde, and our wholehearted approval.

Three years earlier, in *My Darling Clementine*, John Ford had celebrated the bright future of a nation emerging from a period of violence and struggle, in the dedication of Tombstone's half-built church and the courtly dance of Wyatt and Clem, another charming symbolic union of Western cowboy and Eastern lady. The restraint, decorum and community focus of that scene, however, stand in marked contrast to our more ambiguous and explosive duet, wherein violence itself supplies the site and form for the expression of attraction between these latter-day frontier types.

7

....

In a brilliant conceit typical of Lewis's witty, thrifty style, the showdowns between Laurie and Bart and Berry Kroeger's seedy carnival owner, Packy, are framed in her dressing room mirror, icon of the noir woman's power. At the outset Packy's diminished image is trapped, dwarfed by Laurie's reflection as she primps for Bart; seconds later Bart's heroic image materialises in the mirror as Packy attacks Laurie; seizing and raising the mirror to throw at Bart, Packy tries to deny that power; Bart's quick draw and shot shatters the glass and Packy, effectively taking possession of Laurie.

Signifier of the woman's narcissism and duplicity, the mirror exposes us to a side of Laurie that goes beyond the coquettish, engaging performer on stage, a hard, fetishised creature, volatile and grasping ('Big money!'). In following Packy to her tent, the film has abandoned Bart momentarily and allows us access to a Laurie without audience, brutal in her judgments on her former lover – 'a two-bit guy'. Her calculating look in response to Bart's suggestion that they marry, as they drive away from the carnival, casts more shadow on Laurie's character. Outside the office of the desert justice of the peace, in response to Bart's confession of time done in reform school, she frankly admits to a wayward life (if not a killing in St. Louis); but she will try hard 'to be good'. Despite such intimations of the *femme fatale*, Victor Young's lyrical score for the 'Mad About You' theme swells as we fade out on an intimate close-up of the lovers' kiss in a classic romantic moment, worthy of their spectacular courtship and of Bart's gallant rescue of her.

As the curtain falls on the first act of our drama, we discern in Bart and Laurie sympathetic characters of romantic and heroic dimensions, however tarnished or flawed. In stature as well as costume – in their independence, courage and marksmanship – Bart and Laurie refer back to codes and traditions of the American frontier. Although we see differences between them – in outlook and experience – we also sense a bond that makes the Production Code shotgun marriage (Kantor's original script presented problems of 'illicit sex' for the Breen office) not at all a compromise of the film's spirit, a cynical satisfying of social convention, but rather, as many marriages tend to be, a mysterious, hopeful and appropriate confirmation of the commitment between two people setting off on life's journey together. Film noir reveals no shortage of couples setting up inevitably temporary households in which they caricature or falsify marriage – *Detour* is perhaps the most brutal example. Here, despite the fraudulence of the Breen Office's blessings, we have a rare instance in the noir canon of the possibility of a real marriage.

8

As with his predecessor, the gangster, the noir hero's need is 'to draw himself out of the crowd'.[20] This desire to rise above the two-bit level,

the need to break out of anonymity and be 'somebody' – young Bart's phrase for how a gun makes him feel – resonates in the American psyche. Most Americans are unaware that their society's emphasis on the pursuit of happiness, on self-fulfilment and individualism, is a minority point of view, at odds with most of the world. Collectivist cultures, wherein loyalty to the group overrides personal goals (predominant in Latin America, Asia, Africa, and the Middle East), have lower economic productivity than the West, but they also enjoy sharply lower rates of crime, homicide, suicide, divorce, juvenile delinquency, alcoholism and child abuse. There is some economic and sociological basis, then, for seeing such behaviours as the price exacted by the success ethic, as a shadow cast by a society driven by the goals of individual happiness and material abundance.

When asked his religion on his deathbed, early Hollywood producer Jesse Lasky is reputed to have answered, 'American'. That such a creed can be unsatisfactory, that its citizens may fail at, suffer from, even disdain, America's promise of the opportunity to compete for the wonderful life, is one of noir's most persistent thematic statements. Its most profound and moving expression comes in Elia Kazan's *On the Waterfront*, in Terry Malloy's bitter judgment on his brother for failing him, betraying him, not recognising that he could have *been* somebody . . . 'a contender'. The claustrophobic setting of the taxi's back seat – as eloquent in its way as *Singin' in the Rain*'s luminous boulevard – and Brando's agonised performance, render the moment a seminal one in terms of the noir vision as a counter-ideology.

Occasionally, the loss of faith, the rejection of the American Dream, is made an explicit theme, as in the neglected *The Pitfall*, where Dick Powell plays an embittered middle-class citizen: 'I don't want to be like 50 million others . . . I don't want to be an average American, backbone of the country.' John Forbes lives in the classic American dream house of post-war merchandising, right down to the lace curtains in the kitchen, the Wheaties on the counter, the all-American wife in Jane Greer, and their inevitably freckle-faced son. But the house is situated in a row of identical tract homes, and Forbes wonders why nothing has happened 'to the boy voted most likely to succeed'.

Noir heroes are often drifters, loners, losers, casualties of the system. *Detour*'s Al Roberts is the clearest example. Although he yearns for success and the good things of life (evident in the alacrity with which he seizes on his benefactor's identity and goods), he has essentially given up, intimidated by the challenge of America, and has internalised defeat. In contrast, John Forbes has bought into the American ideal – that hard work and playing by the rules can lead to success – and is thoroughly disenchanted by the routine and mediocrity of his life. Cold to his little boy and indifferent to his wife, Forbes's impulse to get in a car and escape it all elicits small sympathy: 'O come on, Wanderlust, you've got a family to support.'

Ironically, Forbes works in an insurance company, icon of capitalism's stability, which in *Double Indemnity* is exposed as a spiritually bankrupt context for its death of a salesman. From the old geezer elevator operator whom the insurance companies wouldn't insure, to Sam Gorlopis, the immigrant trucker who burns his truck for naught, to Keyes, the sour and lonely middle management of the Pacific All Risk Insurance Company, to his strutting and incompetent supervisor, the son of the company's founder, the image of American business and life created in the film is consistently bleak. The most telling moment comes when Keyes offers Walter a promotion to assistant claims manager. Keyes is pitching the job as a holy pursuit in the ethical life when Phyllis calls, breathlessly rehearsing plans for the murder of her husband. Walter wants no part of hard work, fair play, a step up the ladder.

Noir heroes inhabit Palookaville, an American shadow-society oppressed and corrupted by a system that colludes in the production of an amoral, dissident citizenry marked by confused and transgressive gender dynamics. In noir, all of America is gun-crazy, the inevitable dark-side effect of a ferociously aggressive patriarchal capitalism fuelled by a violent national history and ideology. In film after film, noir implicates the capitalist system in a dark poetics that ironically and totally eluded HUAC and the McCarthyite guardians of Hollywood's politics. *Gun Crazy* is exemplary in this regard, also featuring the use of a company as a paradigm of capitalism. The couple's ultimate 'job' will be a robbery of the Armour meat-packing plant, represented in the mythic terms of the film as a house of death and Temple of Capital, whose upper echelon and inner sanctum are contemptuously penetrated by Bart and Laurie's Trojan horse masquerade as workers so that they can steal the payroll, in the process Laurie killing off her busybody supervisor, the dragon-lady who guards the gold.

9

....

Our own couple's pursuit of the American work ethic never leaves the ground. Lewis was an editor before he became a director, and it shows in the construction of a bravura montage of less than a minute's duration and just nine shots, into which the couple's idyllic honeymoon, ominously representing practically the whole of their normal life together, is collapsed. With tongue in cheek, the film rhymes the purchase of a ring for Laurie with its pawning seven brief shots later, the puncturing reversal deflating the dream of the romantic couple posed against geysers and waterfalls in the intervening shots. These tableaux are naive, banal, stilted in their utopianism. Postcards, process shots, the images suggest a separation between the couple and the bright vistas beyond, an air of unreality confirmed with the late-night visit to a depressing highway diner where Bart and Laurie wolf down their meagre dinner. The same couple idealised seconds earlier in pastoral images like advertisements for the good American life now slump in their counter seats, the wide-angle lens stretching and squeezing the cluttered narrow traincar structure, and holding Bart and Laurie far from their

'Postcards, process shots ...'

greasy hamburgers frying in the foreground. Laurie looks grumpy and frumpish, unattractively scratching her nose, irritated with herself for taking on Las Vegas; Bart looks weary. Sadly, they don't have the extra nickel for onions.

As with the film's opening, the extreme compression gives the montage a serio-comic, exemplary flavour. Murphy's Law – or Noir Law – is always operating: whatever can go wrong, will go wrong. The couple are back where they started. The brief circle described here and the straight-ahead speed with which it is closed encapsulate in miniature the up-and-down emotional world of *Gun Crazy*, its roller-coaster trajectory expressed through the dominant motifs – at once formal and thematic – of speed and circularity that organise the film. The lovers will soon take to the road and charge forward like gangbusters – or gangsters, rather – spinning their car through dizzying getaway turns, in a headlong narrative design marked by rings and rolls, curves and carousels, a progress that will insist finally on looping back on itself, with Bart and Laurie returning to the carnival, Cashville, the mountains.

The ups and downs of the couple, going from honeymoon hikes to diner stools, are underlined by a score that swoops upward in full-blooded fashion as the couple climb, then trickles weakly from the diner's radio during Bart and Laurie's hamburger meal. *Gun Crazy* has one of those great old-time Hollywood thematic scores that Robert Altman satirised in *The Long Goodbye*, wherein John Williams accompanies almost every scene with the basic melody arranged and orchestrated differently, even, at one point, as door chimes. Our song is Victor Young's 'Mad About You', written for the film with lyrics ('How I love the enchantment of it all') by Ned Washington. Weaving its way through the film's action and amplifying its emotions, this classic romantic tune provides an apt aural correlative for a film so obsessively focused on a couple so obsessively focused on each other.[21]

10

In their cheap hotel room, Laurie complains, 'What a joint. No more hot water', but Bart sees the bright side: 'Well . . it's a roof, at least.' If Laura and Bart are an impossible, inevitable marriage, it is because they embody the collision that underlies film noir between American populism and European existentialist ideology. As incarnated by Dall, Bart's openness and charm represent the 'good guy' qualities often seen as basic to American character, and to the success of its citizens as they persevere in negotiating its social and economic systems. (Have a nice day.) In the yin and yang of their union, Laurie's lack of faith in principles, people or systems makes possible 'action' – scheming, cold-blooded, ultimately violent behaviour – fully expressive of the dark side of human nature. Laurie recalls *Shadow of a Doubt*'s Uncle Charlie: 'What's the use of looking backward? What's the use of looking ahead? Today's the thing – that's my philosophy. Today.'

The tragedy of Bart and Laurie is that each represents the other's shadow, and that if Bart offers Laurie a bad girl's chance to be good, he also undermines it with his own conflicted nature, his fascination with the gun and everything it represents. This duality is another reason their paradoxical attraction makes sense, for together they complement and complete each other, embodying the full human spectrum of behavioural options and potentials. And it is this conjunction, this dialectic, that resonates in *Gun Crazy*, and that produces in Bart and Laurie the image of an America vividly expressive of the contradictions and complexity of its history and character. Or, as 1960s activist H. Rap Brown put it: '. . . violence is necessary. It is as American as cherry pie.'[22]

11
. . . .

The violence of *Gun Crazy* was, of course, a major concern of the Breen office. Any script that involved young people and guns was to come in for vigilant scrutiny – 'glamorisation' was to be avoided. In keeping with this concern, the film's *mise-en-scène* evidences a wary distance throughout, the shot never allowed to pause on the weapons the couple use.

One of the few scenes Trumbo invented from scratch displays this nervousness, pulling back immediately from a case of handguns to a medium shot of Bart squinting through a gun barrel, Laurie exiting the bathroom behind him. Wrapped in a white floor-length terry-cloth robe, obviously naked beneath but with the high collar up, Laurie looks young and fresh-faced, sans make-up, certainly 'decent', as Gilda would say. In this, the film's authors were perhaps responding to a Breen office caveat that there be 'care in the selection and photographing of the costumes

3 8   'It's too slow, Bart.'

162-19

and dresses for your women', and that 'intimate parts of the body – specifically the breasts of women – be fully covered at all times.'[23] With rods and boobs thus under control, one would think the amount of damage possible to the public's morals in such a scene would be minor indeed.

How will they pay the rent? As they begin to argue, Laurie sits on the bed behind and to the side of Bart, and proceeds to pull on stockings, the robe chastely in place. The route of hard work, opportunity and merit – 'that job with Remington' – is dismissed out of hand. Forty bucks a week is not for Laurie – 'it's too slow, Bart' (one stocking on). She wants 'to do a little living' and, she philosophises, 'if I can't get it one way, I'll get it another' (second stocking). Meanwhile, never looking directly at Laurie, Bart is repeatedly inserting and withdrawing a brush deep into the long-barrelled revolver he is cleaning. If this sounds inordinately suggestive, there is no highlighting, and Laurie, now stepping into her bedroom slippers, circles to the other side of Bart to light a cigarette. She leans on him, still at his guns, from behind, speaking low at his ear, a Sateness fresh from the bath: 'When are *you* going to begin to live? Four years in reform school, then the army – I should think they'd owe *you* something for a change! What's it got you, being so particular?'

The moment is a crucial one in the progress of the couple, one that ironically inverts the Western's logic, the man pleading for peace, to hang up his guns, the woman declaring that 'she has to do what she has to do'. This turbulent yet delightfully domestic scene gradually builds its psychological intensity with cinematographer Russell Harlan's camera making modest adjustments to allow us to contemplate Laurie's artful moves and Bart's desperate attempts to escape, the shot running nearly ninety seconds before cutting in close-ups of Laurie – the good American wife nagging her hubby to show some ambition, to be 'a guy with spirit and guts'.

In agony, Bart makes his stand – he will sell his guns. Laurie plops onto the bed, her bedroom slippers audibly dropping to the floor. 'Kiss me goodbye,' she instructs Bart, for she will be gone when he returns. 'Let's finish it the way we started it – on the level.' Laurie delivers her ultimatum coolly, taking a drag on her cigarette. Bart slowly moves to the bed, putting down his gun case, the shot leaving him to track in to an extreme close-up on Laurie's tense face, her mouth open, nostril flaring, as Bart's face re-enters the frame and inches closer to her, until they come together with what seems like magnetic force in a passionate kiss. We then dissolve to a bowl of gumballs which a gunshot immediately explodes; Bart and Laurie are pulling their first job.

Production Code approval for *Gun Crazy* was granted on 9 September 1949, 'issued upon the understanding that in all release prints . . . the scene of Dall and Cummins kissing on the bed will be the one in which you blur and fade out.'[24] Some local censorship boards, their imaginations presumably over-stimulated by the erotic atmosphere and fetishist overtones of the guns and black stockings, were less forgiving; Maryland, Massachusetts, Ohio and Pennsylvania all required cuts, the last trimming just the embrace on the bed, the first three 'all views of Laurie on bed beginning with and including her following spoken line: "Come on, Bart, let's finish it . . .".'[25] Did the censors see a smutty pun in Cummins's invitation to end it 'on the level'? If so, Lewis, who prides himself on his good taste, maintains none was intended.[26]

12

A commonplace of what we may term the normative film noir pattern is the victory of its designing woman over the weaker male. A Circe, the woman exploits her sexuality to manipulate the hero. Most vividly, we may recall *Out of the Past*'s Robert Mitchum looking up at Jane Greer on the dark Mexico beach as she begs him to believe her, and his reply as he pulls her down: 'Baby, I don't care.' We may see a similar kind of vertigo affecting Bart in his Faustian moment in *Gun Crazy*. Laurie is a spunky, formidable player, tougher than Bart in the high-stakes poker of their relationship. However, as she kisses Bart, how are we to see her own, undeniable passion? The ambiguity of the moment is further extended by the edgy scene's comic climax, the slow rhythm of the building conflict abruptly collapsing (like Bart) in the kiss, and the inspired transition of the exploding gumball bowl, a hilarious symbol of sexual pop and a highly ambiguous comment on Bart's maturity – is this a farewell to childish things, or more showing off?

Many films noirs have such *blanc* moments. The entry in Silver and Ward's *Film Noir: An Encyclopedic Reference to the American Style* refers to *Gun Crazy*'s 'grim narrative', but in common with many other classic noir works, the tone is often humorous.[27] If the gangster genre is a decisive source, behind the dark mythology of film noir, and often looking over its shoulder, there is also the screwball comedy, and its bright optimistic world which noir seeks to deny. Among others, Paul Schrader made the point that the war and the positivist national ideology it required of Hollywood interrupted a working through of the effects of the Great Depression. There is certainly in noir considerable overlap of important elements from the earlier decade and genre, and *Gun Crazy* is absolutely representative in this regard. An aggressive, independent heroine, the deviant couple caught up in sexual intrigue and combat, romantic love seen as erotic madness, a social context stressing conformity and regulation, the innocent pastoral world/corrupt city antinomy, the focus on the common man – these are some of the key features of this continuity, albeit as seen through noir's lens darkly.[28]

Correspondingly, the encroaching shadows are already visible in both Capra and Sturges, who are hardly the opposites orthodox film history posits (Bazin labelled Sturges 'the anti-Capra'). If they are the gods of screwball comedy, Capra and Sturges are also the patron saints of film noir. Capra's fixed linear narrative trajectory inevitably requires its heroes to suffer the fall and crucifixion before they can be redeemed, the term 'Capracorn' hardly fitting the bleak, increasingly harrowing struggle against corrupt, overwhelming forces. Sturges's high-velocity narrative strategies doom his heroes to describe futile concentric circles or desperate ups and downs, the aggressive wit and slapstick conspiring at the humiliation and defeat of his characters. In their respective masterpieces, *It's a Wonderful Life* and *Sullivan's Travels*, their heroes – Capra's attempting to escape the life of the average American, Sturges's to find and study it – are both plunged into sustained nightmarish episodes, forced to suffer the noir fate of death in life, becoming non-persons devoid of selfhood. It is but a short step from these characters and their trials to *Double Indemnity*'s Walter walking outside his apartment after the murder ('I couldn't hear my own footsteps – it was the walk of a dead man'); or *Detour*'s hero trudging in the dark, identity-less, like a zombie; or the grotesque fate of the blackly comic *D.O.A.*'s hero, one minute suppressing crude wolf-whistles, the next hearing: 'I don't think you fully understand, Bigelow. You've been murdered.'

The line of descent from screwball heroines to noir's spider women is equally direct. If we strip Capra's professional women of their jobs and Sturges's gold-diggers of their conscience, we discover noir's dark ladies. Behind Stanwyck mesmerising Fred McMurray with her anklet is Stanwyck bringing a tortured Henry Fonda to near-fainting in *The Lady Eve* as he kneels trying to fit evening slippers, all straps and gaps, on her stockinged feet. In the same way, behind the attempts of Laurie to nag the placid Bart towards a more ambitious and adventurous life we may sense the Tom and Gerry of Sturges' *The Palm Beach Story*, the dissatisfied wife who 'wants it now while I can still enjoy it', threatening to break up with her slower spouse who is instructed that he has 'no idea what a long-legged gal can do without doing anything'.

13

Bart and Laurie's career as gangsters is essentially presented through three robberies, graded in terms of escalating violence to mark the growing conflict between them. In the Hampton Building and Loan job, Laurie clubs unconscious the cop who comes along as she stands guard outside the bank. The robbery of the Rangers and Growers Exchange features Laurie thwarted by her partner in her impulse to fire on a pursuing bank official, while the impotent Bart will deflate the tyre on a cop car giving chase only after her repeated haranguing. The Armour meat-packing plant payroll robbery will go like clockwork until Laurie kills two employees.

However, the film's tone does not darken appreciably. The high-speed getaways, together with the scenes of the couple in transit, shape *Gun Crazy* as a road movie, the constant movement and furious action a graphic expression of their nomadic life together and its illicit pursuit of happiness. Binding the couple more closely, even as it increases the tension between them, the structure of the journey gives the film forward movement as well as the formal purity and spareness of the classic Western. If the journey lacks a destination, its 'high gear' pace obscures this, as well as the couple's total isolation, their speaking to almost no one apart from each other – but for exchanges on the job – from their goodbye to Packy until their return to Cashville.

There is also a distinctly comic flavour to much of the action. A lot of amusing role-playing goes on, with us invariably on the inside and enjoying the joke, as with the middle-aged Lothario (whose Cadillac the couple confiscate) chagrined at Laurie's petite hitchhiker pulling a big gun out of a small purse – Who's got the phallus *now?*, seems to be the punchline. Ingeniously, the Hampton robbery finally allows the duo to play-act cowboys for real, the Western outfits providing rodeo performer cover and allowing them openly to carry weapons. The Rangers and Growers job has them exiting on the run in top coats and dark sunglasses, oddly striking given the flat, overcast day – self-consciously playing movie gangsters now.

The most clever and elaborate performance is as Armour employees in order to pull off an inside payroll job. The humour here, as in many of the couple's impersonations, contains an element of mockery. That Bart and Laurie can become employees in order to plunder the company is an act indicative of the greatest contempt. Bart has spoken as if he yearns for a normal life, but here he is getting his kicks play-acting the ordinary worker, in order to steal his day's pay. Bracketing the different jobs are little screwball vignettes, the couple on the road wittily disguised – like Gable and Colbert as quarrelsome bozo couple in Capra's *It Happened One Night* – as Sunday school teachers, a military family, a go-westering couple. It is Ozzie-and-Harriet impersonations such as these, kin to Norman Rockwell's icons, that contribute to the film's shrewd, impudent bite. In the schizoid throes of finding so much to like in a routine genre piece, the *New York Times* critic finally faulted its stars for looking too much 'like fugitives from a 4-H fair', failing to realise that the expressive power of the film is enhanced by these appealing performances from such fresh-faced players as criminals.[29] As Jack Shadoian put it, Dall and Cummins 'are not screen personalities and must create who and what they are from scratch', the vaulting ambition of our small characters for the big score nicely expressed by actors who were themselves looking to move up in their own careers.[30]

Each of the robberies is further differentiated by being staged from a different perspective. The Hampton robbery positions the audience in the middle of the back seat of the stolen Cadillac, looking over the couple's shoulders as they drive from the outskirts into downtown Hampton. No indication of destination is given, but the intensity of their focus is suggestive, albeit qualified by the domesticity of their chat. They notice how crowded it is and speculate about parking . . . Bart gives Laurie, her hands firm on the wheel, a puff from his cigarette . . . tells her where to turn . . . 'Look out for that rock' . . . they park and Bart exits –

'little screwball vignettes'

'Here goes nothing!' The shot locks us inside the car, the robbery happening offstage, our focus on Laurie and the meddlesome cop who materialises, the shot dollying forward to frame them as they talk on the sidewalk. With Bart's exit the couple take off in high gear, sparks flying between them as they bicker, working off the fear and tension. The second robbery gives us even less warning, the couple on the run from the Exchange as the scene opens. Shot largely from Bart's point of view, the scene plays like nightmare, all clanging alarm bells and dizzying turns. The mad pace and pursuit, Laurie's harsh demands, his agonising dilemma, combine to establish a sense of the chaos inside Bart, a character at the end of his rope and at odds with his partner.

After observing both these jobs from outside of the actual robbery, each of them somewhat sprung on the audience, we are provided with the most careful preparation for the Armour job, including a blueprint plus a run-through. The robbery itself then takes us into the company step by step, cutting back and forth between Bart and Laurie at the outset with the balanced parallel editing that typically frames the couple. For all the differences, however, the strategy remains the same, to keep an unwavering focus on Bart and Laurie, a tightness of identification that precludes any judgment.

14

The Hampton robbery, one of the most celebrated examples of the sequence-shot in all cinema, absolutely forces our participation. This legendary shot, which records the entire hold-up in a single take that runs some three and a half minutes, gives us the vantage point of a member of the crew – of both film and hold-up – from which we can root for the success of the operation. This subversive inclination is all the more encouraged by our growing suspicion that success here – by characters and film-makers – seems, we sense, dependent on the relatively spontaneous performances of two feisty actors being tested by an uncontrolled situation rife with chance and risk of failure. Because the bold and decisive *mise-en-scène* is transparently at the service of the robbery, an effect enhanced by the unity of real and story time, its originality and brio colour the heist itself – the performance of the film and the performance of the crime become one.

In the script the scene ran four pages and eleven shots, plus suspense inserts as needed. Of course it was Lewis, an old hand at staging elaborate long-take action moves in the studio, who had the ingenious idea of a one-shot *tour de force*, which he first rehearsed on 16mm with stand-ins:

> We had a big stretch-out Cadillac. We took all the seats out. We knew we couldn't get a dolly inside the car. So one of the technicians came up with the idea of taking a 2 by 12, putting axle grease on it, then placing another portion of a 2 by 12 on top of it, with protective sides on it so it wouldn't slide off. We mounted the camera on a high-hat [a platform about three inches high] and put a jockey saddle behind the camera for the operator to sit on.
>
> The soundman, who sat in the back of the stretch-out, had portable equipment, including microphones the size of buttons, placed at various points inside the car. On top of this bus, two soundmen, strapped to the luggage carrier, held fish poles with mikes attached. When John and Peggy got out of the car, the soundmen swung the mikes over to get the dialogue.
>
> We had the script girl, the head grip, the cameraman, soundman, myself, everybody squeezed into the back of that car, while John and Peggy sat in front. We didn't make any dry runs at all. Everybody was instructed as to what we were going to be doing. We started a mile out of town. John and Peggy knew the intent and content of the scene, improvised their own dialogue, and generally played it by ear. For example, they didn't know where they were going to park. I wanted it that realistic. It so happens, a car pulled out as they drove up. Otherwise she was going to double park. We made two takes . . . [used] the second one. Off-screen there were people that yelled, 'They held up the bank, they held up the bank.' It was so real and none of the bystanders knew what we were doing. We had no extras except the people the policeman directed. Everything – cars, people – was there on the street.[31]

The high point of both the film and the pair's criminal life, the robbery in all its efficiency cements our impressions of the two as a Hawksian team, professionals under fire. As if this were not enough to keep our sympathies intact, however, Laurie's salacious looks back at us as she checks the pursuit complete the subversion of any possible judgment, rewarding us for our complicity. The outlaw life excites Laurie, her eyes and mouth working, her body leaning against Bart. We have already seen in earlier scenes the admixture of the violent and the erotic. This metaphor is decisively developed further here, Laurie's aroused expression immediately casting a retrospective influence over our perception of the crime, recasting our experience of its gradual build-up, sustained excitement and explosive climax in sexual terms, and deepening our understanding of the couple and their relationship.

The approach in the Armour robbery is equally exhaustive and compromising. Here, however, our privileged accompaniment of the couple provides us with a tour of the company, a rehearsal of the success trajectory dear to capitalism's myth, and a worker's acid analysis of it. As in *Double Indemnity*'s representation of American society through the Pacific All Risk, the Armour Company can be seen to be a systematic expression of the life that the characters reject. Bart's progress through the meat-packing plant not only lays out the job's topography, it also serves as a caricature of the ideal of social mobility enshrined in the capitalist trajectory, as he moves up from the ground level zones of manual labour and production work to arrive at the white-collar, management and money levels. His progress is of course fraudulent, subversive, an act of naked aggression against the work ethic. Bart and Laurie's performances are an attack on the average and the normal, on America, capitalism, fair play. Their last 'job' mocks America's basic unit of honourable labour – a job of work. They trespass, they transgress, they are cowboys still.

The depiction of the normal is bleak. As Bart's co-worker tells him, 'You'll never get rich around here.' Nor is a marital relationship an economic solution: 'Don't fall for that. Do you know how much it costs for two to live? Just twice what it costs for one.' At the next level, the success of Bart's scam for penetrating the payroll office, – delivering steaks to management – speaks volumes about his and the bamboozled guard's nudging knowledge of the privileges of power.

Laurie's boss, Miss Sifert, played by Hollywood's stereotype of a battle-axe, Anne O'Neal, adds to the picture. Her upbraiding of Laurie for wearing pants seems a clear message to be a woman, rein in your independence and ambition, and if you work at it you could be like *her*.

The aging Miss Sifert, prissy and frumpish, coded as unsexual and frustrated, is the loyal 'company man' who is shot down for her trouble. In contrast, if Laurie recalls a World War II Rosie-the-Riveter type, nothing could be more appropriate. If the noir heroine carries the 'screwiness' of the screwball era, that spark and energy, into the darkness, it is because she signifies the complex questions surrounding gender and role that arose in the social upheaval of post-war America.

The final word on this normal world is made poetically by the extraordinary shots of Bart and Laurie rushing past row after row of the huge, lifeless meat carcasses hanging in the darkness of the Armour warehouse. According to its director, the use of the meat plant in *Gun Crazy* was seen as a wonderful opportunity to entertain an audience long accustomed to wartime rationing.[32] Difficult to believe, given these extraordinary, gloomy images of a rigid, functional and cold-blooded world, the products and icons of capitalism. Ominously, the dark tone created here is further extended by the persistent jangle of the alarm bell that gooses the couple as they flee, never diminishing despite the distance.

'The products and icons of capitalism'

15

Bart and Laurie's second robbery had originally been scripted by Kantor to feature Bart exploding light fixtures over employees lying on the floor, but the scene might be rejected, the Breen office had warned, so the production would be well advised to shoot 'some protection shots, merely showing them leaving'.[33] Adopted for the Rangers and Growers heist, where Bart and Laurie exit on the fly, the suggestion accorded well with *Gun Crazy*'s benchmark quality, its fast-moving, compressive, iconic style. Synecdoche – the part for the whole, less is more – defines the film's unique character, the end result of the process of progressive

refinement which the project underwent in evolving from story through scripts to screen. And the Production Code contributed to the distilling of Kantor's ambitious material, suggesting numerous cuts and changes in an attempt to restrict the heroic scale of the outlawry, to avoid the couple taking on a dangerous glamour.

If *Gun Crazy* often evokes the Western, and at times plays like screwball comedy, the censors saw only the film's gangster action. They had found Kantor's 'a very worrisome story . . . which, by its very nature, must inspire sympathy throughout, not only for the criminal, but for his *criminal acts* as well' [original emphasis].[34] Although ahead of its time in its eroticising of violence, the original Kantor script agitated the censors more for both the multiplicity and the graphic portrayal of its crimes. Earlier, the Kings had managed to slip *Dillinger* past the Breen Office, since Monogram had not been a signatory to the embargo forged between Breen and the MPAA in 1945, amending the Production Code to preclude films 'dealing with the life of a notorious criminal of current or recent times'.[35] Raiding *You Only Live Once* for footage of its spectacular rain-drenched bank robbery, the thrifty producers had made a highly profitable little movie, offending official Hollywood in the process.[36] Now the pesky Kings were back, out of line again, outflanking the Code by developing Kantor's story of a rural lad's drift into the gangster realm to exploit the outlaw-couple narrative. And if the project did not glorify a larger-than-life Little Caesar type, it presented the reverse problem: these were the kids next door.

Because imitation by the audience was its greatest fear, the Code required that anti-social acts and violence be kept to a minimum. Such a policy could backfire, as Lewis points out concerning Laurie's killings: 'So when she shoots the guard and he drops, that was done so quickly it's really an illusion.'[37] If we do not see the carnage, is it real to us? Bart's acceptance of Laurie's bloodshed in part derives from its being an abstraction. One reason the dead cop in *Breathless* makes so little impact on our view of Michel is that Godard, who dedicated the film to Monogram and has him quoting *Detour*'s hero – 'My goose is cooked!' – immediately cuts away from our glimpse of the cop falling into bushes.

Ultimately, however, what agitated the Breen office about *Gun Crazy* was that it lacked a strong 'voice for morality'.[38] Their difficulty was to square a narrative centred on a young criminal hero with the

Code's absolute prohibition of sympathy for 'the side of crime, wrongdoing, evil or sin'.[39] The problem may have been an intractable one, given the absence of a strong countervailing force in pursuit of the couple or a regretful past-tense narration acknowledging wrongdoing *à la Double Indemnity*. The best the censors could do was push for the construction of Laurie as villainous, conforming her to the evil temptress stereotype, and recuperate Bart, depicting him as corrupted by her powers. There needed to be 'a greater recognition on the part of [Bart], himself, for the career of crime into which Toni has led him'.[40] In discussions and memoranda, Breen's people forged an agreement with the Kings and Kantor that Bart would be the 'unwilling victim',[41] and went so far as to suggest that lines by Bart about the 'next job' should be given to Laurie.[42] Slanting *Gun Crazy* away from gangster conventions and towards the classic noir syndrome of indicting the aggressive female, the Breen office were speaking with the morality and voice of He-Who-Must-Be-Obeyed, a Zeitgeist that reverberated with masculine paranoia.

5 2   The hold-up scene from the Rangers and Growers robbery, a casualty of the censors

16

. . . .

The harmony of the successful Armour job is shattered once Bart has read the newspaper: 'Two people dead . . . just so we can live without working.' The fear crazes Laurie: 'I can't even think – I can just kill.' Bart will not hear of their trying to separate again: they go together, 'maybe like guns and ammunition go together.' If Laurie is the shooter, Bart is the planner – together they also make up a complete gangster – and now he arranges for escape to Mexico. He wants a ranch, kids, a normal life.

Talk of a family and Mexico sit oddly; it is an impossible combination. In the reactionary ethnic coding that runs through film noir, Mexico, Rio and other Latin locations are invariably the sites of abandon and treachery. The cultural coding of noir as social myth enshrines the paranoia of its alienated white hero in an insistent stereotyping of racial and ethnic minorities as signifiers of the dark shadow-world into which the hero is drawn at his peril. In these terms, film noir – black cinema – is inescapably racist, the marginalisation of 'other' cultures embedded in its dramatic and visual language. 'It's just Chinatown, Jake.'

That Laurie is an English Annie Oakley is curious. A Canadian in Kantor's story, she was obviously made English to accommodate the casting of Cummins. In any case, most commentators on the film have found her as American as the diner's frying hamburgers. If anything, her Englishness seems to add a slightly imperial touch to her claims on the American birthright, and to the high-speed nature of her pursuit of 'action'. In general, the main players in noir are rarely coded as ethnic minorities or of immigrant origins. Indeed, the hero's weakness results in part from the blurring of cultural difference, one source of the alienation being the absence of individual ethnic culture. Secondary characters who signal the noir world, as with *Double Indemnity*'s Sam Gorlopis whose insurance claim is rejected because he himself has burned his truck, or controlling characters – *The Big Heat*'s Lagana and *Night and the City*'s Kristo come to mind – are more the rule.

Kazan's *America, America* provides another perspective in its depiction of the epic noir odyssey of Stavros, the Greek immigrant whose obsession to reach the land of opportunity drives him to play out the role of *homme fatal*, a sex object and site of deception, jilting one woman and serving as gigolo for another; to unbearable compromises and the humiliation of keeping his 'honour safe inside' him before he finally lands triumphantly in America to start life at the bottom as a shoeshine boy. Some triumph; the question, ever ambiguous and conflicted with Kazan, is whether it's all worth it. Is America, America the promised land? Or is it the 'Old Country', the fatherland? As with Terry Malloy in *On the Waterfront*, is the journey towards the light – or the darkness?

Stavros's desire to be *American*, his exhausting struggle to gain entry and find purchase on the capitalist work ethic, throws ironic light on so many noir characters who, like Laurie and Bart, are prepared to steal and kill to avoid working. The pessimism of noir constructs a very different image of America – a work ethic that is too much work, an out-of-reach success, a melting pot into which not only racial but ethnic minorities as well did not always melt, or only very painfully, an America fearful of diversity, and a time when ethnic frictions, cross-cultural conflict, shame over origins, and distrust of immigrants, were strong currents in American life.

17

Originally Laurie's plan had the couple separating after the Armour job, raising the spectre of her betraying Bart. Our doubts – and Laurie's too – are gloriously allayed, however, when the two discover separate cars, separate lives, are not a possibility, each circling back in an impulsive duet described by the two convertibles, the vehicles reined round like horses, the balance and rhyme of their original meeting reaffirmed here in the parallel action and editing, the mad, spinning vertigo of their life together slowed, their graceful 180-degree turns binding the two in a ring that their two halves of a circle make up, Bart vacating his car to join Laurie in a passionate embrace, a romantic epiphany, the image transcendent in its crowning of the two with golden sunshine haloing their kiss. A triumph of *mise-en-scène*, the moment wittily marks the summit of the couple's passionate commitment to each other in vehicular terms – what could be more American?

Ironically, however, the lovers' inability to separate will result in a doomed love, authorities tracking them to the carnival where they celebrate their planned escape to Mexico with another euphoric romantic moment. If the formal values of the car duet evoke and reaffirm their 'marriage', the visit to the carnival dance hall sadly rhymes with their honeymoon in its brevity, slaphappy utopianism and sudden reversal. This looking back to happier times is ominous, given the couple's situation.

The complexity of tone is present immediately in the shot of Bart and Laurie helpless on the wildly descending roller coaster – speed, again – that begins the brief montage of their night out. If this mad up-and-down journey with Bart clutching Laurie has been their life, the film seems to say, then the next shot, the gentle rise and fall of the carousel, the amused cowboys on separate horses that describe gracefully sedate circles round-and-round, up-and-down, is perhaps their future.

As the couple buy their tickets for the carnival's dance hall, we hear another vocal orchestration of the Young–Washington 'Mad About You', this time as a dance tune, and it continues as we dissolve to the couple on the floor. In the carnival when they met they had been the show, on stage above Cashville's citizenry. Here, they are lost in the crowd of ordinary people, their desire expressed through the wholly traditional convention of the slow dance, as opposed to the isolating theatrics of the fast draw. As 'their music' plays, they circle again and

On the roller coaster

again, dancing close. They are lovers. The music swells, a clarinet trilling, and the band's leader rises with violin, the camera tracking past him to settle on a close shot of the fair young woman who begins to sing sweetly, sincerely, as the band segues into:

> The crowd sees me out dancin',
> Carefree and romancin',
> Happy with my someone new,
> I'm laughing on the outside,
> Crying on the inside,
> Cause I'm still in love with you . . .[43]

Like the diner and the convertible, the big band/girl vocalist and romantic slow dance are quintessential icons of post-war 1940s America. Bart and Laurie joining the dance here signals their attempt to cross back into the daylight world of mainstream America, to join, symbolically, with Wyatt and Clementine, to no longer live a Janus life that harbours a violent, dark nature beneath the nice guy, good neighbour facade. The song's theme of laughter and tears also evokes the twin theatre masks of comedy and tragedy, apt signifiers for their life together, as well as for the range of the film's emotional tone.

It is Bart and Laurie's supreme moment as a couple. As if enchanted with love, they celebrate their success, their union, their destiny. The knowledge of past killing, the sharing of responsibility for the blood shed, has not rendered their marriage false, a wedding stained by blood, a bond of lust and death, an anti-marriage; they do not join Walter and Phyllis and all the other noir couples doomed to self-hatred and mutual destruction 'right down the line'. They are transfigured by their love; each sees their whole life as a preparation for the perfection of this moment. They are serenaded by a young, vital feminine Cupid, a veritable songbird of love warbling with tenderness and warmth, pluck and innocent faith, a dimpled fresh-faced icon of American purity and idealism that crowns the moment, and speaks the couple's transcendent love for each other.

This dreamy, moony moment is a classic example of classical Greek drama's 'false dawn', the tragic protagonists lulled by the cruel gods (or goddess, here) into a treacherous anticipation of a sunny outcome, which proves, alas, a mirage; the darkness of the long noir night has not lifted. This radiant woman, the goddess of blanc America, the bobbysoxer

queen, sings not for them. How could she? The lady represents those
values – openness, sincerity, a lack of guile – ripped off by the couple in
their impersonations. She presides over the gates, the daylight world's
answer to *D.O.A.*'s black 'jive' underworld kings, and they are closed to
Bart and Laurie.[44] The couple are not innocent. The evil beneath has not
been washed away (the 'crying on the inside') by their new pact. The
hubris of their affront to the normal world – the Armour masquerade and
robbery, the dead guardians of capital – bars them.

Once the couple step out of the building, they immediately
discover the reality – authorities have traced the Armour currency, have
been to the hotel, are *here*. They flee back into the hall and, as the music
continues (minus the thrush's song) and the couples sway, undertake a
sad reversal of their just completed romantic journey, joining the dancers
now in order to hide as they slip across the floor, visibly out of step and
against the flow, casting circumspect glances in all directions, reborn as
fugitive criminals, a poignant, painful, pathetic comeuppance. They
sneak out of the door into the classic noir coding of a long, dark,
shadowy corridor, and the omens that echo the film's opening, wherein
Bart first fell, multiply. We see them reflected, trapped, in a plate-glass

'A dimpled fresh-faced icon of American purity'

window, they run desperately, nearly falling out of control, Laurie drops her fur, the street is inevitably wet. Bart pulls Laurie into a darkened taxi; the couple have been cast into the shadows.

18

Returning to Cashville, the couple look through a window in at the bright kitchen scene of Ruby, Bart's sister, and her children intimately framed by the window panes. The shot pauses over Laurie's blank gaze, a vertical shadow-line bisecting her face. The ambiguity is sustained in her reaction once the couple, incongruous in their dressed-up yet dishevelled state, have entered the tidy Flagler home: 'Gee, what cute kids.'

So open and bright a town is Cashville, so normal, that drawn shades and closed blinds, the idea of a darkened home in daytime, are enough to signal the presence of the noir virus to Dave and Clyde. The arrival of Bart's boyhood chums flushes Bart out, gun drawn, to stand on the porch, looking across at them in the yard where, over fifteen years earlier, he had fired his only kill-shot. They carry no weapons, stand there in their neat uniforms, hands relaxed at their sides, smug in their rectitude, the guardians of Cashville – 'Bart, this is our town. We don't want any shooting or anybody getting hurt.' Inevitably, they have become social engineers, like the judge whose earlier banishment of Bart they now repeat. Bart seems to sense the condescension and veiled hostility, and leaves, ignoring their suggestion that the couple should surrender.

The hostility between the normal and the deviant worlds is insisted on in Bart and Laurie's stay in Cashville. Indeed, how could a community named after the highest value in American capitalism ('cash-money', as immigrants were wont to call it) condone the return of its least favoured son, he who had begun his criminal climb on their very own main street? Clearly, Ruby resents Bart's violation of her home, the 'disgrace' her brother has brought on her family. There is not a spark of affection, of sibling feeling. Between Ruby and Laurie there is open warfare. The film's coding is absolutely and insistently generic here – Ruby in her white blouse and checked apron, cooking in the service of her family, the suspicious Laurie leaning casually against a cupboard in her black dress, doing her nails, staring. Nurturing archetype, woman as redeemer, versus the spider woman, the *femme fatale*. That Laurie should presume, monster-like, to abduct Ruby's baby to barter for the couple's safety would seem to provide a final measure of this hostility, and of Laurie's absolute evil. There is no ambiguity about this act in the script: returning the baby to its playpen, Bart gives Laurie a look 'worse than a blow'.

However, this judgment is not in the film; instead, another close-up on Laurie's face, stony, blank, staring straight ahead as Bart fires the engine. Unlike her older sisters in the outlaw-couple cycle, Laurie is not allowed pregnancy, the fur wrap she has had to abandon serving as the film's emblem of a life's desire for 'things – a lot of things'. Beneath that hard mask and the bright idea of taking the baby, however, are there the stirrings of a bleak envy, an inchoate desire for what might have been, might still be, the road not taken? Similarly, is Ruby's rage simply the result of her disgrace? Or is it in part fuelled by bitterness at her life's mockery of the period's ideal of the dream home and family, her life of drudgery while hubby is off on a business trip in San Francisco, presumably having a drink with *D.O.A.*'s Bigelow?

In any case, the humanising undercurrent that runs throughout *Gun Crazy* in Cummins's complex performance can certainly be said to be at work here, the idea of abducting the child hinting at something

'But he'd be safe. They wouldn't dare ...'

more than a simple, breathtaking act of evil. What makes *Gun Crazy* so arresting at the dramatic level, adding depth and mystery to the film, is Peggy Cummins's successful resistance to the reduction of Laurie to stereotype – against the chauvinist conspiracy of traditional aesthetics and morality to 'put the blame on Mame' – and her representation of the character as a site of contradiction and conflict.

19

In filling out the review forms required by the Production Code approval process, Breen's administrators had defined the end of the film as 'moral' (other choices were 'happy' or 'unhappy'), and in answer to whether the film elicited any sympathy for its criminals, had judged: 'Yes and no. Some sympathy generated for John Dall, none for Peggy Cummins.'[45] The matter, of course, is not that simple; once the duo meet it is not so easy to divorce them for purposes of measuring audience commitments. In fact, the whole point of the film is that together they make up a phenomenon far greater than the sum of its parts.

There is a resonant shot that comes late in the film, at the outset of the snowbound couple's discussion of their future. Looking out of the Montana coalshed, Laurie appears vulnerable, sad, bored, the effect heightened by the two icy tear tracks positioned beneath her eyes on the window. This curiously affecting image is, however, immediately subverted by a roller coaster of a discussion that jerks our belief in Laurie up and down – yes, she agrees, it's time to quit the banditry, *but* they need one more job; then they'll be together forever, *but* they'll have to separate to escape. While insisting on their passionate union, *Gun Crazy* simultaneously holds out the possibility of Laurie's betrayal of Bart, of a kind of schizoid Laurie, a Laurie in flux.

At once unscrupulous and innocent, loving and manipulative, sweet and fiercely resentful of authority, hard as nails yet feminine to the end, Laurie communicates the contradictions we associate with true personality rather than the fixed identity of a movie type. If she lacks stable values and is driven by a pursuit of sensual thrills and high living, her commitment to Bart can nonetheless be read as a serious attempt to resist the lure of a lifetime's logic and conditioning, to try, as she puts it, 'to be good'.

Kantor's original script had proposed a much darker couple who actually *do* kidnap Ruby's baby, punishing Laurie by having her precede her partner in a horrible death, run over by the disc harrow of a farmer she had wounded. Trumbo had saved her from that fate, preserving her for the couple's last stand. However, directions in the final script still described her at extreme moments as having 'the look of a killer' and 'the eyes of a cobra'. Interviews with the director record his agreement with the idea of Laurie as a mythological essence: 'A beautiful demon who [*sic*] no man can resist.'[46] A written note in the director's copy of the script also reads: 'Shoot ending (alt.) of Laurie killing Bart who stands in front pleading not to shoot at Dave and Clyde. Both endings.' We can be thankful for small favours. Such a change would have tilted the precarious balance of sympathy even further away from Laurie. As it is, we can see an absolute logic in the united front of authors and censors culminating in the 'dignified' new title – *Deadly is the Female*.

'Come on, honey,' says Bart, moving off and holding the hand which clutches her purse straps, the line delivered with a solicitude light years away from the mockery of Phyllis helping her paramour-killer ('Good luck, honey') make his train in *Double Indemnity*. They go deeper into the forest, down a narrow stream tunnelled over by bushes, Laurie pitching forward face-down into the water, her falls – like the hanging slabs of dead meat and the roller coaster – hinting at what lies ahead. Night comes on as they stop by a tree, staggering and visibly exhausted; Laurie is finished. 'Let them come – I kill them! I kill them.'

Laurie's fear is traumatic, her loss of self total. It is possible to see in moments such as these Laurie's own victimisation, her aggression a logical response to a hard, damaging life. Laurie's skill with mirror and black stockings, her ability to use her 'self' as bait to trap and manipulate, the element of malicious pleasure ('Have a nice time in California'), all suggest a hostility driving her, a rage born of life under men, life needful of men, which she vents on Packy as she moves to a stronger consort, and which erupts violently against the masculinised Miss Sifert and the oppressed housewife, Ruby. Laurie has said she's been kicked around; there is an element of payback in her actions.

As Clyde and Dave relentlessly approach, insultingly ignoring her – it is all Bart, Bart, Bart – she becomes increasingly agitated, hysterical, catatonic. In moments like these she loses herself, she is beside herself.

The underlying paradigm for the noir hero is the character who lacks self-knowledge, the lost self. The purest condition of this is the amnesiac – Oedipus is the first noir hero. Amnesia and split personality have been the explicit subject for a number of noirs (including Lewis's *So Dark the Night*), Hitchcock's *Spellbound* the *locus classicus*.[47] However, it is in a later Hitchcock film, *Marnie*, that we find another heroine who takes pleasure from using her self as a lure, a disturbed personality whose sexual pathology stems from the sexual abuse ('Make him go, Mama') visited on her as a child. Do Laurie's fear and rage also flow from the threat of those who would take 'legal possession'? Both women take pathological erotic satisfaction from the violation of others' rights, space and property, both take fetishistic pleasure in wittily appropriating the disguise of conventional costumes and demure demeanours. And, of course, both women suffer from attacks of psychosis at moments of extreme stress. Reading against the grain of unfriendliness in script and censors, as I have, it is possible to see in Laurie's trance-like state at moments of disabling fear the sign of violation, her person its site, resulting in her own compensating violent aggression and her violation of the body politic.

I would argue that such a reading is infinitely more suggestive than seeing Laurie as monstrous psycho, more in keeping with a title which erects the sign of troubled patriarchy over the film's action, and the logical outcome of the film's parallelism in its depiction of the couple, given that Bart is also the victim of disturbed masculinity. Such a reading is also supported, I believe, by the range, nuances and complexity of Cummins's extraordinary performance. If Laurie finally remains unfathomable, I prefer seeing her mystery as a sign of humanity, rather than tired proof of her spidery qualities.

20

An intelligent and demanding actress who had behind her a distinguished juvenile career at Ireland's Abbey Players and extensive work on the London stage and in British cinema, Cummins did not fare well in Hollywood. Miscast in the plum lead role of 20th Century-Fox's production based on the best-selling sex saga *Forever Amber*, she suffered the ultimate disaster of being replaced, but soldiered on and appeared in five films during the next three years, none bringing her star status or critical recognition, before happily seizing on *Gun Crazy*. Cummins had strong ideas about her roles. She spoke of a possible production titled *Waltz into Darkness*:

> . . . a wonderful title. The girl in that even plots murder. What I feel about all these roles is that they have a provocative element and are more interesting than straight heroines. They give the actress a chance to surprise her audiences, and they are better for me to play because I am the type I am physically. There is a kind of dissembling about them, a double edge that is different, that keeps entirely away from the obvious.[48]

Cummins chafed throughout her career at limitations suggested by her petite and pixieish looks, and regretted not having dropped Peggy for Margaret: 'It sounds like a girl who is strictly for light entertainment. It wouldn't sound right, would it, to have Peggy Cummins as Lady Macbeth?'[49]

One wonders what Hitchcock could have done with her. It was, however, with *Gun Crazy* that Cummins bid Hollywood a ferociously spirited goodbye, returning to England and some fifteen productions, many of them innocuous comedies, before retiring. *Gun Crazy* is undoubtedly her lasting achievement, providing this intelligent actress with the finely tuned sense of image her decisive opportunity to deliver a huge performance, to waltz into darkness and play her Shakespeare, the echoes of which the sharp reviewer in the *Los Angeles Daily News* was quick to spot: 'Like Lady Macbeth she captivates her new husband and involves him first in an array of bizarre stick-ups . . . the story is Miss Cummins uses the Shakespearean taunt it takes guts for crime to get her lover rolling on their new career.'[50]

21

. . . .

Earlier, we had picked up their flight from Cashville with a graceful panning shot that follows them through a climbing curve. It is the kind of shot that in a Raoul Walsh chase, as in *High Sierra*, would be almost immediately followed, metronome-like, with a matching shot of the pursuit past the same landmark. However, Lewis's intense focus stays on the couple, in the familiar frontal and over-the-shoulder two-shots, followed by balancing low-angle close-ups of each of them, Bart's framed by the steering wheel, separated by a vertiginous point-of-view shot travelling forward.

The formal values of the ascent into the mountains recall the earlier getaways, the dizzy turns and high speed. The conventions of the American action film are orchestrated here at their most expressive. The visceral experience offered the audience expresses a way of life, a *modus operandi*, ultimately a philosophical system. The excitement and risk of Bart and Laurie's high-stakes gambling, the elevation of the odds, the steepness of the bet and the extremity of their plight are created directly through the dynamism of Lewis's *mise-en-scène*. The editing of their rush up the mountain and past the obstacles of road crew and checkpoint fragments the run, maximising our experience of their peril. Unbalanced exterior shots of the car labouring upwards, point-of-view shots capturing the mad rush forwards or flirting with the lip of the steep curves, are intercut with tense interiors of the couple, in steep low-angle shots up from the floor.

We see here the model in action, and of action, that so attracted Godard and his *nouvelle vague* compatriots to the American cinema and its genres. It is but a short step from sequences such as these to the intellectualised B-movies of Godard and Truffaut, to Belmondo blaring off in his stolen American hard-top convertible – 'Pa-pa-pa-pa–Paaaa-trizia!' – down the long French highway to his rendezvous with destiny in the form of a highway cop. Robert Mundy was the first of many critics to point to the possible influence of *Gun Crazy* on Godard, especially in the tonal values of the escape, all sunglasses and trenchcoats, from the second of the couple's bank jobs.[51]

Russell Harlan, who had shot a decade's worth of low-budget Lesley Selander Westerns, and two years earlier on *Red River* had begun what would prove an equally long association with Hawks, consistently served Lewis well. Seeming to thrive on the rugged challenges of location work and Lewis's often elaborate staging demands, Harlan's cinematography is vigorously expressive and resourceful. An example in the couple's flight through the mountains, capturing their growing desperation, is the shot through a dark bush's branches – Laurie's first fall comes here – which then tracks with the couple in their breathless dash forward, the speed and panic communicated subliminally by the

invisible match of three jump cuts which bring us progressively closer –
to the couple, to Laurie, then to Bart, before Laurie finally calls a halt,
breathless. A magisterial 'shot' (we experience it as continuous) that
kinetically captures their mad forward energy through dark, obstructing
branches and bushes that crowd in on the camera, forcing it to tunnel
through an overbearingly close, hostile world – the kind of effect that
Kurosawa was eliciting raves for in *Rashomon*, also released in 1950 –
would be overlooked here. As with the films of Walsh and Hawks, the
expressivity of the style is so pure, the employment of action to define
character and situation so efficient, that the mastery of these codes and
conventions can largely go unrecognised, invisible.

22

. . . .

'When it's daylight . . .', Bart had said. But ominously, the couple
are shrouded in fog – a signifier of noir's menace and mystification
at its most powerful. It is in fog, mist, smoke or steam that the heist will go
bad (*Criss-Cross*), the hoodlum will buy it (*T-men*), a life's promise will be

In the fog

Detoured. Breaking with the open-air location style of the film, Lewis's decision to use a fogged-in studio set brings *Gun Crazy* to grim closure.[52] Huddled in the hellish fog, Bart and Laurie have but seconds to live.

Standard accounts of the end credit Bart with shooting Laurie to protect his boyhood chums. Nothing, in my view, could be further from the truth. Bart dispatches his love to protect her from herself, and the shedding of more blood. It is an act that indeed makes the end moral, although perhaps not in the Code's terms. 'Laurie – no matter what happens . . .' The tender last-minute pledge of love, a convention of couple-on-the-run movies, is followed with a final kiss, interrupted as Clyde and Dave – icons of Law and Order – announce their presence. Defenders of the status quo, they march forward, disembodied, secure in their invulnerability, their patronising voices echoing in the fog ('We're coming in, Bart . . . you're not a killer, Bart'). Sons of their fathers, smug in their normality, Clyde and Dave can be seen as the golden boys of America (Trumbo had them both graduating from Stanford), heirs to and defenders of a benign capitalism.

In shooting Laurie, Bart is not casting a vote for these hollow men, these robots, over and against his passionate bond with Laurie; rather he is reaffirming that bond. Hamlet-like, irresolute to the end, ambivalent in his love affair with the darkness, Bart resolves his dilemma with a final, reluctant embrace of 'action'. Playing off and parodying the Western, *Gun Crazy* builds inevitably towards the final showdown, the most venerable of the Western's rituals, which Bart ironically revises and redirects by killing his soul mate, an act of love, his only true kill-shot a kind of killing of himself; capitalism's production for use, at last. Chekhov is said to have remarked that if a gun is introduced in the first scene, it should fire in the last. Here again, *Gun Crazy* proves a film that adheres to first principles with great purity – and, of course, the lethal shot ironically balances and answers Laurie's flirtatious 'killing' of Bart when they had first seen each other.

Their bodies lie together, Bart's slightly beyond Laurie, their heads in tandem describing a perfect diagonal line, Bart's face typically open to the sky, Laurie on her side, an enigma still, her face covered by her hair. As the theme, scored as a tender lament, commences for the last time, Clyde and Dave approach, and Clyde delivers an epitaph – 'Yeah, we're all right' – smacking of self-pity and pseudo-bitterness. Zombies, pods, automatons, they turn and begin their lock-step march away and the shot cranes back and up to a cosmic perspective on the fog-shrouded funeral bier, the music culminating in a strident heavenly choir, the end title zooming towards us from vanishing point with the same boldness and energetic authority as the main title had at the outset. Our understanding of the proceedings is unambiguous – the scene is that of a double suicide, the air one of mournfulness.

Pace our Los Angeles critic, the tone is less that of *Macbeth* – 'Of this dead butcher and his fiend-like queen' – and more that of:

> A glooming peace this morning with it brings.
> The sun for sorrow will not show his head.
> Go hence, to have more talk of these sad things;
> Some shall be pardoned, and some punished;
> For never was a story of more woe
> Than this of Juliet and her Romeo.[53]

23

By refusing to develop the quirks and contradictions in Bart and Laurie and their relationships, *Gun Crazy* positions them halfway between psychological types and American icons. This split makes the film frustrating, yet finally resonant and ambiguous – as we have seen with the enigma of Laurie. If many noir films can be seen to have poetic elements, in *Gun Crazy* the mythic undertones are much stronger because of the film's iconic and exemplary approach to action, setting and character. The purity and balance of the narrative give it an allegorical feel. The couple, although humanised by virtue of their split, conflicted nature, remain heroic types. Often, the world created suggests an archetypal quality, a universe peopled by emblematic characters, Elizabethan humours such as the judge and the clown, white and dark wisdom incarnate. The young Bart's Promethean rebellion, his encounter with dark forces, the acts of skill, the raid on the meat-packing plant's Death House of Capital, the exile to the Hades-like swamp – much of the narrative can be seen as dark fairy tale. Self-conscious stylistic elements, such as the narrative's clarity of progression, the rhyming scenes, insistent framing and self-reflexive staging, enhance this effect of abstraction and detachment.

These archetypal elements feed into and sustain the film's relationship with the Western. In particular, the mythic structures throw into relief the importance of the couple's magical skill as marksmen. Bart employs his prowess to 'free' Laurie twice; her use of the weapon is invariably deadly. It is this power that ignites their passion and sets the couple apart. Together with their ability to live by their wits, this expertise is what makes them interesting to us: they are the inheritors of the mythic skill of the Western hero. However, this charismatic power, making them rivals to 'the gods', is also the sign of disturbance. The skill is unmanageable – neither can control it. They are both 'gun crazy'.

The gun is the central icon of the film, as it is of America. Guarantor of liberty? Or tool of licence? If guns are America's cross – a notion suggested by the image of Bart with arms flung wide, as if crucified, in front of the six-gun he is about to loot – it is because they reverberate throughout its history, as Kantor's sound montage was designed to suggest. The gun is the signifier of freedom, an always loaded issue in a country where there is only so much success to go around. As Laurie says, what have 'they' done for Bart? Should he sell his guns? Or use his skill with them as an equaliser?

The film identifies this prowess with the Old West. Behind the rampage of the Barrow and like gangs that terrorised mid- and south-western 1930s America with their high-speed robberies and killings were the earlier model of Western bad 'men' on horseback of the 1870s – Jesse James, Billy the Kid and Belle Starr. Bart and Laurie's dress in Western regalia at the outset, together with Laurie's stage persona which joins Annie Oakley, the legendary sharpshooter, and Starr, the West's most famous female outlaw, insist on this legacy, and on their status as motorised cowboys. The 'fire' that Bart and Laurie release is the free-wheeling, rapacious spirit of frontier America, its 'how the West was won' individualism and adventurism. It is the entrepreneurial energy of the Wild West, the pulse of Daniel Boone and early settlers pushing over the Appalachian Mountains, the mountain men and trappers, the pony express and the railway builders, the ranchers and rustlers, the Indian wars, the gold rush and the 49ers, the bandits and bad men.

Like the actual use of the gun, this freedom, the film suggests, must be regulated in a more advanced society ('We all want things, Bart'). However, for Bart and Laurie, the liberty promised its citizens in America's manifesto is that of Liberty Valance, the right to 'take' liberties.

There is nothing romantic or Robin Hoodish about this. Apart from their skill, Bart and Laurie are like the very people they prey on. What would Capra's George Bailey – Bart's alter ego – have to say about their raids on the small-town savings and loans companies they target? It is altogether appropriate that a production still of the second bank job has them looking monstrous, vampiric, in their charge out of the door, the large dark sunglasses – shades – signifiers of their dissociation, their schizophrenia.

Bart and Laurie take, and take pleasure in the taking. We see especially in Laurie that it is erotic. The violence and the sex are intertwined – *Gun Crazy* is shameless in catering to our baser nature. They rip off society, and get off in the process. There is the suggestion of violation here; our outlaw couple screw society. The myth of the Western hero, the character with a code who redeems the community, is decisively and radically subverted.

Despite its numerous and prominent references to the Western, most critical accounts of the film have largely downplayed this motif in favour of the more sensational marriage of sexuality and violence that *Gun Crazy* flaunts. However, in my view what gives *Gun Crazy* its centrality in the classic film noir cycle is its insight into the role of the Western myth. It makes clear that the frontier spirit and the American work ethic are by no means synonymous, that the pioneer mentality, the freedom so crucial in exploring a new land, the nomadic impulse to trek over the next hill, become in film noir the basis for the trajectory into darkness, the impulse to escape the ordinary and to wander. Indulging a personalised Manifest Destiny translates into becoming the victim of romantic fatalism, the dark passion that drives the action of so many noir works.

This dynamic helps to explain the privileged status of western settings in film noir – in particular, the dark cities of Los Angeles and San Francisco, archetypal noir sites. The westward journey, the open road, the cowboy style, speed – these are the cultural icons of America's past and present ceaselessly recycled to reassure us that the frontier is still open. Is America's fascination with guns, its gun lobby that clamorously protects a nation which has reportedly two hundred million guns in circulation against the regulation and 'control' of waiting periods, registration, and bans on assault weapons and armour-piercing bullets – institutionalised madness, gun craziness? Or is it an expression of the ideology, guaranteed by the constitution, that created and shaped America, America? The Golden Gate Bridge, the nation's and San

Francisco's most famous span, offers a similarly ambiguous extension of the frontier in its refusal to erect barricades – fences – with some 1,000 (known) souls who have indulged their freedom, their desire, their vertigo. In noir, the geography becomes psychic, the quest turning inward towards the frontier of the self, defining the dark boundary beyond which to travel is to fall.

24

Gun Crazy's great qualities are its clean lines, the clarity of its focus. At the same time, the film benefits from echoing and combining elements of three of Hollywood's most popular genres. The mix of romantic couple, Western style and gangster aggression creates a spontaneous semiological combustion of signs and meanings, a film of great depth and poetic reach, for all the modesty of its scale.

Bart and Laurie often resemble a screwball couple who have innocently wandered into the noir world waif-like, orphans in the storm. Their love of guns is a sign of their flawed nature – their turbulence, isolation, need for power. They are nice kids who have gone bad, short-sighted and soon overmatched against an unforgiving, increasingly corporate and technologically sophisticated society. Their journey is small-time epic, their moment of freedom brief. The film looks forward to an America that will be increasingly preoccupied with and needful of youthful rebellion, speed and action, even as it becomes increasingly uncertain of role and direction, traumatised by an escalating loss of innocence. The constant shots of the couple on the road – one of the film's binding visual motifs – reflects the already developing love affair between Americans and their cars, citizens who will increasingly get their kicks from Route 66. However, the freedom that the film sings of is not simply that of the open road, and certainly not that of innocence or achievement, but freedom through crime, a disquieting message from America's heartland.

Classical in its form, subversive in its point of view, *Gun Crazy* is B-movie poetry, B-movie tragedy, B-movie movie. A film in the American vernacular of action form without a single personal centre, it nevertheless synthesises into a cohesive, highly disciplined work. *Gun Crazy*'s production clearly benefited from a confluence of forces –

ideological, economic, aesthetic – that worked towards formal conciseness and refinement. Maligned on occasion as achieving only a few great set pieces, the film is in fact remarkable in sustaining a concentrated flow of wit, energy and creativity. One of the lessons that Godard learned from Hollywood cinema was that all one needed to make a movie was a girl and a gun, an essentialist approach basic to the King Brothers' philosophy, level and style of operation. Its marriage in *Gun Crazy* to a modestly upscaled budget, a thoughtful script and a vital director and cast resulted in an exceptionally focused work of human scale, iconic reach and fast footwork.

If *Gun Crazy* is one of the most winning of films, it is in part precisely because of its lowly status. The 'B-movieness' of small noir such as *Gun Crazy* or *Detour*, and its effects on the audience, can hardly be ignored. In economic terms, the classic position of the B-movie on the lower half of the programme defined it as a bonus, a freebie, a gift – like the plates, cups and saucers the post-war audience collected on attendance from week to week. This status made excusable the frequently shoddy quality of the production, and its often shameless catering to the audience's baser instincts. Without waxing too nostalgic about how the movies back then belonged to 'the people', it is possible to suggest that B-movies in particular often provided a modest pleasure for post-war working and lower middle-class audiences, and that part of that pleasure arose from, not in spite of, the gross limitations of the form.

The extreme economy and compression that characterise *Gun Crazy*'s style can be said to represent the B-movie ethic *par excellence*, the guiding principle of a maximum of meaning for a minimum of means. It is often a sense of surplus value, of more bang to the buck, that makes B-movies a low-class, populist pleasure. When the result, as here, is also a breathtakingly good film into the bargain, then the sense is positively one of stolen pleasure. In 1972 Paul Schrader declared *Gun Crazy* 'one of the best American films ever made'.[54] Pauline Kael, on the other hand, sees it as a film of 'fascinating crumminess'.[55] If we are overly concerned with the film's cheapness we must find such a claim as Schrader's absurdly extravagant. At the same time, if we dismiss the cheapness as simply a condition of production, we will miss the unique match of the film's means and message which is a key source of its power.

The visible absence of glamour – Hollywood's signifier for American abundance and the success ethic – provides a source of great visual pleasure in *Gun Crazy*, keying our awareness of the appropriately crummy proportions of the personnel and proceedings both to the unpretentious scale of the heroes and to the modesty of their threat to the established order – rather like the threat the Kings were posing to the DeMilles and Goldwyns with the film. The MPAA embargo on traditional gangster films had undoubtedly opened the door to projects focused on criminal behaviour by a more familiar, smaller scale of hero. The availability of the often tawdry pulp fiction format of the B-movie, and the comfortable symbiotic relationship it offered unglamorous stories centred on working stiffs and drifters, provided a form made to order. The tendency of noir to be peopled by mid- and low-level stars – the John Dalls and Tom Neals – played into this dynamic of normalisation. The Bogarts and Mitchums often stay above the sordidness, are less in keeping with noir's roots in the Great Depression, are too much star figures.

Small films noirs like *Gun Crazy* were thus ideally equipped to frame the portraits and annals of ordinary men going down to defeat. However tarnished, these protagonists – typically pursuing self-interest rather than the common good – can nonetheless be said to achieve a measure of nobility in their doomed efforts to navigate an irrational, nightmarish world. Although up to no good, noir's black sheep often perversely display the courage and know-how typical of the good guys of heroic culture – as with Bart and Laurie's Hawksian skills – albeit in the service of a mobility very different from that enshrined in capitalist ideology. Film noir represents an attempt to restructure and codify heroic myth, to speak to the alienation and weakness of a citizenry feeling increasingly divorced from stable social structures. We share the pain of Joe Average as he stands looking at the woods, lovely, dark and deep. The heroic nature of noir characters lies precisely in their refusal to keep promises and accept their humdrum journey. Erring in their hubris in trying to rise above themselves, these small-time tragic figures bring down an often disproportionate payback. The effect can be ambiguous, but often – as with *Gun Crazy* – the films can be read as the Production Code's worst nightmare, normalising the uncertain self, the unexamined life, deviant and subversive behaviour, passion over reason. Hence the film's tonic effect and immense popularity, its underground appeal lying precisely in its going against the American grain, celebrating a couple with no appetite for duty, honesty or work. Depicting a dark America of bleak horizons, *Gun Crazy* nevertheless achieves a great élan and liberating spirit, a singing in the rain all its own.

Some accounts of the film warn that it is so good that it would be wrong to overpraise, that its flaws should not be overlooked. More generous is the judgment that by the highest standard the film falls short, that at its centre there is a vacuum that arises from eschewing psychology and over-reliance on action. However, it has been my argument that the film's 'anti-Americanism' is all the more expressive for the spontaneity and unselfconsciousness of its evocation. *Gun Crazy* is a low-cost example of how Hollywood's habit of speaking to the typical, average American can give rise to an allegorical resonance and force, and release creative energies and effort that finally lift the production to a transcendent level of achievement.

25

There is poetic justice in the King Brothers' *Gun Crazy* having achieved the status of a Hollywood classic. The Kings were actually the Kosinskis, classic Horatio Algers, the sons of Russian immigrants who had grown up in Los Angeles shining shoes and delivering newspapers, before moving as teenagers into bootlegging and then pinball, slot machines, and 'soundies', the Hollywood Talkietone arcade projection cabinets. Going to Cecil B. DeMille for advice, they had been unimpressed and set out to 'do it better'. They were to hunger for respect throughout a spectacularly successful poverty-row career, in which they produced some eighteen movies during a thirty-year run dating from their 1941 goldmine debut film, *Paper Bullets*, later reissued both as *Crime, Inc.* and *Gangs, Inc.* Given that crime movies were the cornerstone of their success, their shady past was too good an angle for the press and the wily Kings not to exploit, stories playing them up as former gangsters, supposedly ready and able to punch people out or do needed stunt work. One account had Frank, the leader, interrupting a mob scene to demonstrate: 'I know. I was interviewed by Capone once.'[56]

A Runyonesque operation – their office the site of craps games, bookies and show girls – made the Kings easy to caricature, as did their tubby Oliver Hardy looks, their home life with the formidable Mama King (ladies' men, they never married), and her reputedly foolproof instinct for good screen material. That material more often than not reflected the rough world they knew. Tough-minded businessmen first, they had a populist soul and personal credo, operating on the assumption that they were 'just common, everyday people and we retain that touch'. As Maurice, the eldest, put it, 'We know what'll be good subjects. We like action and movement and psychological mysteries – close to life, though.' They went into everything 'with action and the gambling spirit'.[57]

Ironically, the low-class Kings were to inscribe themselves within Hollywood's history as one of the catalysts in the breakdown of the Blacklist. If they operated initially out of a sharp self-interest in employing banned writers such as Trumbo and Edward Dmytryk (*Mutiny*, 1951), it must be remembered that in contrast to the craven majors the independent Kings stood behind Trumbo as the pressure mounted following his covert winning of the Oscar. We should also note that it was through the good offices of Maurice King that the Academy finally delivered the prize to Trumbo in 1976 in his twilight days.

Despite their upscale moves and accomplishments, however, the ambitious Kings were locked into their déclassé B-movie mould. If

(l. to r.) John Dall, producer Frank King and Peggy Cummins

Trumbo's Academy Award-winning story for *The Brave One* finally brought them a measure of prestige, it is appropriate that *Gun Crazy* is the capstone of their career. Although they have been invisible in previous accounts of the film, it is impossible, given their close involvement with their projects and strong personal ideology, not to see the Kings as the final piece of the authorship puzzle that surrounds *Gun Crazy*. Like Bart and Laurie, Cummins and Dall, Kantor, Trumbo and Lewis – these blue-collar millionaires had their share of struggle, frustration and failure. The alienation from an official, mainstream America, the felt need to 'break out' – the grand leitmotif of American film noir and *Gun Crazy*'s dominant subtext – may well have spoken in various ways to all its principals, as it has to its many appreciative audiences over the years. *Gun Crazy*'s production provided the site for the personal effort and vision of a number of authors, all of whom it ultimately escaped, a small film with a collective soul.

POSTSCRIPT: 24 August 1995

I swing off the British Rail train from London onto the platform at Cooden Beach and immediately spot Peggy Cummins. On the phone when we had arranged our meeting, her vivacious, witty style had prompted a flirtatious suggestion – should I wear a rose so that she would recognise me? If you like, she had replied, maybe she too would wear something – guns, perhaps? When it comes to it, however, we are the only people on the platform, and she is in any case unmistakable, tiny still, chunkier now, but the hair, gone silver-blonde, is in the same style, and when she smiles the Laurie-voltage is still there, the years fall away.

Robust and active as she nears seventy, she swims in the ocean regularly, Cooden Beach the last stop before Bexhill-on-Sea, not that far, she tells me, from Brighton. I remind her that Laurie had been given a Brighton childhood, and she is amused to be reminded of the production's transparent efforts to account for her largely non-existent accent. Briskly piloting her Honda Shuttle – a far cry from the big American cars she loved driving in the 40s – she soon has us at the home where she and Derek Dunnett, whom she married after *Gun Crazy* was in the can, now reside, a short block from the beach, having given up the nearby farm of forty acres that was their residence for many years. There is a flat in London, a son and daughter and grandchildren, a busy, full life.

On the phone she had been incredulous that Britain's National Film Archive was planning to strike a new print of the film for preservation. 'Isn't that something,' she had mused, 'isn't that something.' I ask her now when she first became aware that there existed a special regard for the film. It was at the National Film Theatre's screening in London in 1985, to which she had been invited, when Lewis had done the *Guardian* lecture.

Asked to what she would attribute the success of the film, she immediately points to the harmony of its production. The Kings, often around, had been supportive, all business. Of course going to work for them had been a distinct comedown, they were looked down upon by everyone – but they had treated her well, and it had been an honour to be in a film based on Kantor's work. The script had been well constructed, solid, 'constantly building'. And the film had been the product of a small unit of people all working to the same end. There were no memos coming down from head office, no one looking over your shoulder. Glaring contrast was provided by her traumatic experience on *Forever Amber*, from which she had been removed. She shows me colour blow-ups of her costume fittings for the film. Zanuck and 20th Century-Fox had brought her to town only to try to change her, giving her a false, lowered forehead and burying her beneath the weight of huge satin dresses. Hawks had expressed interest in working with her on *Amber*; she wonders how things would have developed with him. But, I ask, what about John Stahl, her original director on *Amber*, and his reputation for women's pictures – *Back Street* and Irene Dunne, she interjects. Exactly, I reply. No comment, she says, those Irish blue-green eyes holding my own in a firm, intelligent gaze. Read this, she says, passing me a note scribbled on three small restaurant bills:

Peggy

I've wanted to write you a note for a long time to tell you not to be *too unhappy* about *Amber* (but I was afraid you would think me presumptuous). Don't be unhappy – take it in your stride – do whatever is given you as a substitution as best you can and make them 'eat their words'.

Good luck
J.C.

Guess, she demands, but before I can decipher the initials she announces – Joan Crawford! – and it is clear that Cummins was touched when she came across the note while foraging through her memorabilia in preparation for my visit.

As I listen to her accounts of Lewis's vigorous, well-organised direction, the free hand she and Dall had had to work by themselves to create their performances, her respect for Harlan, a wonderful cinematographer, and the dismay expressed by the Kings at the copious smears of mud she had gleefully applied to that tiny, porcelain-like face – I realise that the world outside the film had been as tight, as well focused, as the diegetic one. It becomes clear how much this small miracle of a film was blessed in its ambition, creativity and maverick spirit by the freewheeling, independent circumstances of its production and personnel. The film-makers had been a very small, congenial group of high-powered professionals on their own out in the country and up in the mountains. Were there many retakes? Not on a 30-day schedule for a movie of that scope. She is surprised that Lewis speaks of two takes of the Hampton sequence-shot, remembering only one, generally the rule, the film largely shot in sequence – a production, evidently, that had

Stars, crew (Madeleine Robinson, Charles Huber) and the Willys 'Jeepster' which provides the set for the most iconic, all-American image of the 'honeymoon' montage

moved as fast as its plot. I am reminded of the story of Welles shouting on his *Macbeth* set, 'Run, don't walk. This is a B-picture!'

She and Dall had got on very well. She speaks of other co-stars – Ronald Colman, Dana Andrews, Vincent Price, Victor Mature. In particular, Mature had been a good friend, taking off her hands two dogs that suitors had given her. No one had ever given her diamonds, she wails, *or* furs – but that was OK, furs being the badge of a compliant woman. I remind her of the fur wrap in the movie, and she immediately blurts '*rat*, you mean fur *rat*', a remembered slur on the Kings' meagre costume budget. In fact, what she wore had been largely left up to her, most of the clothing her own, the terry-cloth bathrobe, for instance – and, yes, the silk stockings had been her idea, had seemed 'right'. And the beret? She had worn berets all her life, as a child and at school, the style had always suited her, the beret in the movie was a 20th Century-Fox item from *Escape*, and it had been her idea to wear it. No one back then had been talking Bonnie and Clyde – 'never, no way' – as Lewis had also told me, puzzled by questions about the hat (Kantor, Trumbo and the Kings, all gone now, might have told a different story).[58]

Back to actors. Looking for the TV news and coming on *The Postman Always Rings Twice*, she had been struck by John Garfield – a model of contained force and intensity. That was what she had tried for with Laurie, to be direct, low-key, in contrast to when she 'blew up'. Derek – a weather eye on the television and England's attempt to defeat the formidable West Indies cricketers – ruefully observes that Laurie had been the only opportunity Cummins had had to play against type. Yes, have your students see *Who Goes There* to get an idea of the contrast, she suggests. She holds no resentment against Fox, but they had not used her well – perhaps MGM would have been a better base. She had always wanted the Bette Davis roles, had been given the Jeanne Crain ones. It is clear that Laurie was one of her most enjoyable roles.

After a wonderful lunch of cold salmon and Guinness, I get down to business. How did she see Laurie? I tell her that, despite the shadow of the *femme fatale* stereotype, there are always students in my classes who see the character as sympathetic, vulnerable, pointing to her look into the Flagler kitchen, her line on entering. I go to the script to quote and we are both surprised when I read, 'What – what nice children.' No, it's 'Gee, what cute kids', she remembers, and how it had been important to her that she read the line neutrally, that the audience should not know what she was feeling because Laurie herself did not know. No, Laurie was not evil, but blinkered, single-minded, maybe not so bright, a person who would do anything to get what she wanted, to keep the party going.

What about an earlier look, I ask, the aroused glance back at the Hampton job? Many people ask about that, she says; as Cummins sees it, firmly decorous, 'the adrenalin is running'. Laurie's hysteria under peak pressure? She's totally conflicted – she wants to shoot, she doesn't want to shoot. Her relationship with Bart? She thought she could control it, but fell in love. Cummins especially likes the car 'duet' scene – 'because the other me comes out, the one who wants to stay.' On *Gun Crazy* being her last American film – 'Yes, I shot my way out.' But she'd have come back, loved America, Hollywood, those heady days.

My train time approaches and Derek snaps some photos of us. But as we move to the door, she stops me – come, see this – and flips open a large album on a stand in the hall. Her wedding pictures, November 1949, just before the release of *Deadly is the Female*. Look, she says, turning page after page of formal portraits of the wedding party, at the centre of which is that angelic, radiantly smiling baby face. 'Look,' she says, almost under her breath and with a hint of awe, 'this is the girl who was Annie Laurie Starr.' I watch page after page go by, and finally ask: 'Is that who you were – a sweet-faced child – or were you a killer?' She looks up at me, flashes that smile, and replies: '*Both* – the same girl played both.'

Peggy Cummins and Jim Kitses, 24 August 1995

NOTES

· ·

1 *Motion Picture Production Code File and Approval Certificate*, No. 14023, 9 September 1949.

2 *Variety*, 31 October 1949.

3 Philip Scheuer, *Los Angeles Times*, undated review, MPAA Academy Library *Gun Crazy* clipping file.

4 Howard Thompson, *New York Times*, 25 August 1950.

5 Second feature co-release was a Lesley Selander/Tim Holt oater, *Storm over Wyoming*. *Gun Crazy*'s director has estimated the budget at $400,000, still a bonanza compared to earlier King Brothers productions released through Monogram such as *When Strangers Marry*, under $50,000, and *Dillinger* (see note 36); Monogram's own productions could cost as little as $16,000. For background on 'nervous A's', see Linda May Strawn's interview with Steve Broidy in Todd McCarthy and Charles Flynn (eds.), *Kings of the Bs* (New York: E. P. Dutton, 1975).

6 Paul Kerr, 'My Name is Joseph H. Lewis', *Screen*, vol. 24 nos. 4–5, July–October 1983.

7 Bob Thomas, *Los Angeles Citizen News*, 16 May 1949.

8 Quoted by Richard Thompson, in Paul Schrader, Robert Mundy and Richard Thompson, 'Joseph H. Lewis: Three Articles, An Interview and Filmography', *Cinema*, vol. 7 no. 1 (Fall 1971), p. 46.

9 Jack Shadoian, *Dreams and Dead Ends: The American Gangster/Crime Film* (Cambridge, MA: MIT Press, 1977), pp. 149–65.

10 Schrader, Mundy and Thompson, 'Joseph H. Lewis', p. 46.

11 Charles Higham and Joel Greenburg, *Hollywood in the Forties* (New York: Paperback Library, 1968), p 19.

12 Paul Schrader, 'Notes on Film Noir', in Barry Keith Grant (ed.), *Film Genre Reader* (University of Texas Press, 1986), p. 176.

13 Quoted in *San Francisco Chronicle*, 25 July 1994.

14 Gustave de Beaumont, *Marie* (Stanford, CA: Stanford University Press, 1958), p. 102. Beaumont and Alexis de Tocqueville toured the USA in 1831–2, pursuing research sponsored by the French government for a report they co-wrote on the penitentiary system in the United States. Both *Marie* and de Tocqueville's *Democracy in America* were by-products of that trip.

15 In his lectures on popular culture; but see also Stuart Hall and Paddy Whannel, *The Popular Arts* (London: Hutchinson, 1964), p. 32.

16 Robert Warshow, 'The Gangster as Tragic Hero', *The Immediate Experience* (New York: Doubleday Anchor Books, 1964), pp. 83–8.

17 Millard Kaufman told me he never saw story, script or film. According to Mitzi Trumbo, her father was amused at the poetic justice of the rumour he encountered on occasion that had him ghost-writing the Kaufman-scripted *Bad Day at Black Rock*. In his *Dalton Trumbo* (New York: Scribner's, 1977), Bruce Cook notes that Nedrick Young, who plays Dave, was also blacklisted and, like Trumbo, would go on to win an Oscar, co-writing *The Defiant Ones* (1958) with Harold Jacob Smith under the pseudonym of Nathan E. Douglas. In his *Guardian* Lecture at London's National Film Theatre (see Bibliography) Lewis suggested that Young had 'worked on' *Gun Crazy*'s script; in conversations with myself he explained that they had discussed the scenario. Lewis has said that his last film, *Terror in a Texas Town* (1958), a ten-day Western shot for $80,000 which brought the director full-circle back to his quickie B-oater origins, was his contribution to bucking the blacklist on behalf of his friend. Young plays a villain who is impaled on a harpoon hurled by Sterling Hayden in the film's bizarre final shoot-out. Trumbo, Young and John Howard Lawson have all been variously credited with working on the script.

18 Jeffrey Richards, 'Frank Capra and the Cinema of Populism', in Bill Nichols (ed.), *Movies and Methods* (Berkeley: University of California Press, 1976), p. 70. Lewis told Danny Peary he cast Dall because he knew a 'gay' would 'betray' Bart's 'weakness' (*Cult Movies*: New York, Delta Press, 1981). This edifice of shaky assumptions evidently rests on the ground of Dall's earlier performance as the

leader of the Leopold/Loeb-like killers in
Rope. In general, however, memories of a
small movie that occupied a brief summer over
thirty (now forty-five) years previously must
be weighed judiciously. The Kings had been
pondering casting options for two years before
Lewis was hired to shoot the picture, and
chose Dall when he aggressively lobbied for
the role by seeking Frank King out dressed and
'postured' like 'a gun crazy kid' (*LA Daily
News*, 5 June 1950). Of the Kings, Maurice was
reputed to be more involved with script
development, Franklin was the executive in
charge of production, and Herman – here
credited as 'Technical Advisor – was more
active on the distribution/exhibition end.
19 Edward Buscombe, *Stagecoach* (London:
BFI Publishing, 1992), p. 9.
20 Warshow, *The Immediate Experience*, p. 88.
21 That the Kings were able to tempt the
A-grade Young away from Paramount's
upscale noir such as *The Big Clock* and *I Walk
Alone*, John Ford (*Rio Grande*, *The Quiet Man*)
and big projects (*The Greatest Show on Earth*,
Shane) is remarkable. *Gun Crazy*'s press kit
informed exhibitors that marketing displays
might feature 'Mad About You', recorded by
Frank Sinatra, Kitty Kallen, Russ Case and
Stuart Foster, and Charlie Spivak and
Orchestra. Other promotions offered the
distaff star of *Deadly is the Female* in
advertisements as a Lux Toilet Soap user ("'I'm
a Lux Girl," says Peggy Cummins'), suggested
special screenings for police, marksmanship
contests, and 'current headlines' lobby displays:
'Hardly a week goes by nowadays without
seeing a story on the front pages concerning the
exploits of some notorious woman.'
22 Christopher Ricks and William L. Vance
(eds.), *The Faber Book of America* (London
and Boston: Faber and Faber, 1992), p. 259.
23 *Production Code File*, letter of 9 June 1947,
from Joseph Breen to Franklin King.
24 Ibid., 'Postscript to Certificate No. 14023'.
25 Ibid., 'Report from the Local Censor Boards'.
26 In conversation with the author.
27 Alain Silver and Elizabeth Ward (eds.),
*Film Noir: An Encyclopedic Reference to the

American Style (Woodstock, New York:
Overlook Press, 1979), p. 118. The plot
summary erroneously has them married before
they are fired by Packy.
28 The interplay between the two forms has
often been remarked on. Crucial to my reading
of *Gun Crazy* is Robin Wood's typically
illuminating 'Ideology, Genre, Auteur' in Barry
K. Grant (ed.), *Film Genre Reader* (University
of Texas Press, 1986), p. 63, where he compares
Shadow of a Doubt and *It's a Wonderful Life* and
argues that 'the home/wandering antinomy is
by no means the exclusive preserve of the
Western'. *Gun Crazy*'s depiction of the young
and the rootless insists that the source of the
dialectic, trans-generic though it may be, is in
the frontier experience.
29 Howard Thompson, *New York Times*, 25
August 1950.
30 Shadoian, *Dreams and Dead Ends*, p. 153.
31 Lony Ruhman, Steven Schwartz and Rob
Conway, '*Gun Crazy*, "The accomplishment of
many, many minds": An Interview with Joseph
H. Lewis', *Velvet Light Trap*, no. 20 (Summer
1983), p. 19.
32 Ibid., p. 20.
33 *Production Code File*, letter of 9 June 1947;
the reference is to the robbery of 'the power
and light company', eventually changed to the
Rangers and Growers Exchange. A still of
Laurie and Bart holding up the tubby bank
official who pursues the couple, kindly lent to
me by Peggy Cummins, suggests that the
interior action was shot.
34 Ibid., letter of 28 May 1947 from Joseph
Breen to Franklin King.
35 Quoted in Carlos Clarens, *Crime Movies*
(New York and London: W. W. Norton, 1980),
p. 192.
36 'In the '40s the studios, all the majors, had
signed a consent agreement not to make
gangster pictures. Monogram was not a
signatory, so Louis B. Mayer was indignant.
He called up [producer] Frank King and said,
"Frank, you gotta destroy the negative of
Dillinger for the good of the industry." Frank
said, "Sure, what'll you pay me?" Louis B.
Mayer said, "I'll pay you nothing." Hell, the

picture cost $65,000 and it made millions. I had a third of it.' Screenwriter Philip Yordan in Doug McClelland (ed.), *Forties Film Talk* (Jefferson, NC, and London: McFarland and Company, 1992), p. 209. In his biography of Trumbo, Bruce Cook has the budget at $193,000, with profits of over $4 million.

37 '. . . for censorship reasons anytime a person got killed we could only stay on long enough to see the shot and that was it. They considered lingering on the victim severe brutality.' Ruhman, Schwartz and Conway, *Velvet Light Trap*, p. 20.

38 *Production Code File*, letter to Franklin King from Joseph Breen, 9 May 1947.

39 Ibid., letter of 28 May 1947.

40 Ibid., 'Suggestions which may be helpful re: "*Gun Crazy*"'.

41 Ibid., 'Memo for Files', 29 May 1947.

42 Ibid., letter of 9 June 1947.

43 'Laughing on the Outside, Crying on the Inside', music by Bernie Wayne, lyrics by Ben Raleigh, 1946.

44 The divine 'danceland singer' credited erroneously as Frances Irwin was actually Frances Irvin, listed as such in the 'Ingenues' section of *The Academy Players Dictionary: 1949* (Hollywood: AMPAS, 1949, p. 100). There is also a photograph in the *Los Angeles Times* of 20 January 1949, captioned: 'NEWCOMER – Frances Irvin, 19-year-old actress from Texas, is a principal in *Tongue in Cheek* . . . revue cast is made up of talented "unknowns".' *Sic transit gloria*. Victim of a typographical error, Irvin is a small symbol of the 'going nowhereness' of our fugitive couple, the film itself, and too many of its players, big and small.

45 *Production Code File*, approval review form, 9 September 1949.

46 Danny Peary, *Cult Movies* (New York: Delta, 1981), p. 121.

47 I am indebted to Loren Means and his paper on 'Amnesia and Film Noir', delivered in a graduate seminar on film noir at San Francisco State University in autumn 1992.

48 Quoted in an article by Edwin Schallert, 'Peggy Cummins Pegs Self for "Evil Lady":

Angelic-featured Actress Likes Villainess-Type, Provocative Parts', in *Los Angeles Times*, 6 March 1949.

49 Quoted by Sheila Graham in the *Des Moines Sunday Register*, 10 March 1946.

50 'Deadly is the Female' by David Bongard, *Los Angeles Daily News*, 27 January 1950.

51 Schrader, Mundy and Thompson, *Cinema*, p. 45. *Vivre sa Vie* and *Bande à Part* are other Godard films that recall *Gun Crazy*.

52 The Kings had originally approached Kantor about 'Passport in Purple', a gimmicky if democratic slice-of-life tale that tracks a book of matches circulating in New York City. Kantor had suggested 'Gun Crazy' instead, pitching it from the beginning as a location movie, and in the spring of 1947 the Kings and their staff had scouted sites in Kantor's Webster City – banks, schools, the local abbatoir. Bad weather was the official reason given for cancelling the summer shoot, but casting and script were more likely factors. Two years later it was a location movie, but not Iowa. The California towns of Montrose and Reseda provided settings for bank robberies, Baldwin Lake Estates and Topanga Canyon stood in for the mythical San Lorenzo mountains, and the Armour plant, if not on a back lot, was conveniently located in 'old Hollywood', on East Olympic Boulevard.

53 Shakespeare, *Romeo and Juliet*, Act V, Scene III, the play's concluding lines.

54 Schrader, Mundy and Thompson, *Cinema*, p. 43.

55 Pauline Kael, *5001 Nights at the Movies* (New York: Holt, Rinehart and Winston, 1982), p. 235.

56 Robert Lewin, 'The King Brothers', *Life*, 22 November 1948.

57 Mary Morris, 'The B-Picture Kings', *PM*, 7 July 1946.

58 Arthur Penn tells me he has never seen *Gun Crazy*, nor (he is certain) had the screenwriters of *Bonnie and Clyde*, and that Faye Dunaway's beret harks back to the original Bonnie.

CREDITS

. . . .

Gun Crazy

USA
1950
US release
As *Deadly is the Female*: 26 January 1950
As *Gun Crazy*: 24 August 1950
Distributor
United Artists
Copyright date
1949
Production Company
Pioneer Pictures Corporation
A King Bros Production
United Artists Presentation
Producers
Maurice King, Frank King
Assistant to the Producer
Arthur Gardner
Production Manager
Allen K. Wood
Director
Joseph H. Lewis
Assistant Director
Frank S. Heath

Screenplay
MacKinlay Kantor, Millard Kaufman [as front for Dalton Trumbo] from a *Saturday Evening Post* story by MacKinlay Kantor
Script Continuity
Jack Herzberg
Dialogue Coach
Madeleine Robinson
Photography (b & w)
Russell Harlan
Camera Operator
Fleet Southcott
Grip
Harry Lewis
Gaffer
Lloyd Garnell
Stills
Ed Jones
Music
Victor Young
Orchestration
Leo Shuken, Sidney Cutner
Song
'Mad About You' by Victor Young (music), Ned Washington (lyrics), performed by Frances Irvin
Music Editor
Stuart Frye
Editor
Harry Gerstad
Production Designer
Gordon Wiles
Set Decorator
Raymond Boltz Jr.
Miss Cummins' Wardrobe
Norma
Make-up
Charles Huber
Hairstyles
Carla Hadley
Sound Engineer
Tom Lambert
Technical Adviser
Herman King

Peggy Cummins
Annie Laurie Starr
John Dall
Bart Tare
Berry Kroeger
Packet
Morris Carnovsky
Judge Willoughby
Anabel Shaw
Ruby Tare
Harry Lewis
Clyde Boston
Nedrick Young
Dave Allister
Rusty Tamblyn
Bart Tare, aged 14
[and uncredited]
Stanley Prager
Bluey-Bluey
Trevor Bardette
Sheriff Boston
Mickey Little
Bart Tare, aged 7
Paul Frison
Clyde Boston, aged 14
Dave Bair
Dave Allister, aged 14
Virginia Farmer
Miss Wynn
Anne O'Neal
Miss Sifert
Frances Irvin
Danceland singer
Don Beddoe
Cadillac driver
Robert Osterloh
Hampton policeman
Shimen Ruskin
Cab driver
Harry Hayden
Mr Mallenberg
Charles McGraw
Ira
Ray Teal
California border inspector

Credits checked by Markku Salmi

BIBLIOGRAPHY

. . . .

The Strange History of Bonnie and Clyde by John Treherne (London: Jonathan Cape, 1984) is an authoritative account of the Barrow gang's exploits and the cult that grew up around it, and includes a look at the film cycle. However, although Kantor's original story was written in 1939, its action was set in the immediate post-World War I era, spiritually closer to Jesse James than to the outlaw couple. Published in the *Saturday Evening Post* in 1940, the story is available in *Author's Choice* (Boston: The Writer, 1944), with its ending of a tearful hero arrested by Clyde – which the *Post*'s editor had forced on Kantor – followed by Kantor's comments and preferred ending of Nelly (as he is called here) gunned down by a posse. Kantor's Iowa childhood is described in *But Look, the Morn* (New York: Coward, McCann, 1947); we are not surprised to find Kantor as a lad 'riven with horror' on shooting a sparrow with his first BB gun (p. 84). Tim Kantor provides inside and ambivalent glimpses of 'a man of note – at one time almost as important in popular estimation as in his own', in *My Father's Voice* (New York: McGraw-Hill, 1988, p. 2).

Although no blow-by-blow record of the script's production exists, three versions of the screenplay

survive. Kantor's original, dated 24 March 1947, is available from the Manuscript Division of the Library of Congress in Washington (DC), which also holds some forty boxes of Kantor's unsorted papers and correspondence. A transitional script, undated but incorporating changes on colour-coded pages dated 17 November 1948, is housed at the MPAA Academy Library in Beverly Hills, which also holds the *Motion Picture Production Code File* on the film, as well as the few files and scrapbooks the King Brothers left behind. This version, at 146 pages, is undoubtedly the script Trumbo refers to in a letter to his agent dated 2 October 1948, anthologised in the very useful collection of Trumbo's correspondence, *Additional Dialogue* (ed., Helen Manfull, New York: Bantam Books, 1972, p. 91): 'Those fellows are hooked, I think. They have a good script and appear to respect me. The final draft goes to them in the same mail that this letter goes to you.' Installing the key structural changes of opening with Bart's smash-and-grab and trial-cum-flashbacks and the finale of the duo dying together, this draft also incorporates name changes (Cottonwood to Cashville, Nelly to Bart and Toni to Laurie), but still retains cumbersome Kantor motifs

such as Bart's love of popcorn, which gives him away when the FBI alert vendors, and a more elaborate final pursuit involving cutaways to panorama shots and pursuers.

The director's own copy of the 'Final Draft Screenplay', dated 5 April 1949 and marked up with numerous staging diagrams and reminders, is on deposit at the Film Center, School of the Art Institute of Chicago, which also holds other Lewis material – scripts (*Retreat, Hell*, TV programmes) and 16mm film. Copies of this draft are also held by both the American Film Institute and the University of Southern California Cinema/TV Libraries. This final draft, again uncredited but in all likelihood the result of more Trumbo doctoring, lops another thirty pages of Kantor's original script, and is not corrected to include changes Lewis made in the shooting – altered lines, the Hampton sequence-shot, numerous touches such as the exploding gumballs and Laurie's donning of her stockings (Lewis, in conversation with the author: 'A nice touch – that was Peggy's, I think').

Dalton Trumbo's papers are held by the State Historical Society of Wisconsin at Madison, also the location of the Wisconsin Center for Film and Theater Research, which boasts the production's abundant still photograph key books. Bruce Cook's *Dalton Trumbo* (New York: Scribner's, 1977) chronicles the screenwriter's association with the Kings, and Victor S. Navasky's *Naming Names* (New York: Viking, 1980) provides a definitive account of the blacklist. See Phillip Kemp's 'From the Nightmare Factory: HUAC and the Politics of Noir' (*Sight and Sound*, Autumn 1986) for an account of how noir's social meanings escaped both Hollywood and its guardians.

A relatively early critical project was the *Cinema* issue (vol. 7 no. 1, Fall 1971) which established in even-handed fashion the uneven nature of Lewis's career, and provided stimulating accounts of Lewis – Paul Schrader seeing *Gun Crazy* as a product of favourable industrial forces, Robert Mundy zeroing in on Lewis's action style, and Richard Thompson making a case for Lewis as a *maudit* specialist, and revealing a maverick preference for *The Big Combo*. These pieces were backed, however, by a career interview by Peter Bogdanovich that invited construction of Lewis as sole auteur, making Kantor the author of a script of 375 pages which Lewis and Millard Kaufman supposedly condensed. This fantastic version of the script's development has been repeated by Lewis in various forms over the

years, Kantor's script even ballooning to 500 pages in a later interview despite the director's apparent generosity as quoted in the title, '*Gun Crazy*, "The accomplishment of many, many minds"' (Lony Ruhmann, Steven Schwartz and Rob Conway, eds., *Velvet Light Trap* no. 20, Summer 1983, pp. 17–21).

In 1972, at a panel discussion which Paul Schrader organised to launch his film noir retrospective at the Los Angeles County Museum of Art with Robert Aldrich, Sam Fuller, Lewis and Schrader, and which I chaired, our director exclaimed in exasperation: 'I have many children – why all the questions on *Gun Crazy*?' Shortly afterwards, he re-cut his point of view: 'I have three favourite films – *Gun Crazy*, *Gun Crazy* and *Gun Crazy*.' Lewis has been interviewed in countless venues and media in both the USA and Britain. In 1985 he enjoyed a tour of European film centres, and on 17 June that year he was interviewed for the *Guardian* Lecture at the National Film Theatre in London by William K. Everson. In general, there is little mention of Trumbo. The official credit change was announced by the Writers' Guild on 27 October 1992, occasioned by the gracious withdrawal of Millard Kaufman.

Lewis's interview with Gerald Peary for *Positif* no. 1712, July/August 1975, is accompanied by an auteur analysis of his noir films by Stuart Kaminsky. Myron Meisel's study, 'Joseph H.

Lewis: Tourist in the Asylum', in Todd McCarthy and Charles Flynn's *Kings of the Bs* (New York: E. P. Dutton, 1975), carries on the *Cinema* critics' fair-minded tone and remains the most sustained examination of the Lewis canon. The McCarthy/Flynn study is an indispensable source on the B-movie generally; Linda May Strawn's interview with Steve Broidy of Monogram/Allied Artists is particularly relevant. *American Directors*, vol. I (New York: McGraw-Hill, 1983), by Jean-Pierre Coursodon with Pierre Sauvage, offers a thorough exploration of Lewis and another dissenting vote for *The Big Combo*.

A retrospective review of Lewis is introduced by Tim Pulleine in the *Monthly Film Bulletin* (vol. 47 no. 554, March 1980, pp. 56–7), whose summary puts well the likely consensus on a film-maker whose career and individual films 'are inclined to be less than the sum of their parts'. In 'My Name is Joseph H. Lewis' (*Screen*, vol. 24 nos. 4–5, July–October 1983), Paul Kerr develops issues explored earlier in 'Out of What Past? Notes on the B Film Noir' (*Screen Education* nos. 32–3, Autumn/Winter 1979, pp. 45–65), as well as in a paper presented at the Edinburgh Film Festival of 1980, which included a Lewis retrospective. Kerr argues for the shaping of Lewis's career and of B-film noir generally in terms of the economic and ideological forces determining change in post-war Hollywood.

Balancing Meisel's film-by-film approach, Kerr provides a wealth of contextual data and a thorough overview both of Lewis's career and the various critical accounts of it. The same *Screen* issue also contains a well-researched account by Janet Staiger of the post-war shift to independent production, 'Individualism versus Collectivism' (pp. 68–79).

Jack Shadoian's account of *Gun Crazy* in *Dreams and Dead Ends: The American Gangster/Crime Film* (MIT Press, 1977) provides the most sustained account of the film read in terms of the ideological struggle between a mad love and a repressive society. This analysis is reprised in psychoanalytic terms by Frank Krutnik in his *In a Lonely Street* (London: Routledge, 1991). The indispensable *Film Noir: An Encyclopedic Reference to the American Style* (eds. Alain Silver and Elizabeth Ward, Woodstock, NY: Overlook Press, 1979) also takes the *amour fou* route. Ed Lowry provides an insightful analysis in *Cinema Texas Program Notes* ('Gun Crazy', vol. 15 no. 3, 29 November 1978). The film also finds sympathetic study (although inflected by typically tendentious Lewis interview material) in Danny Peary's *Cult Movies* (New York: Delta Press, 1981).

Janey Place's essay in particular, and the groundbreaking collection of the same title in which it appears, *Women in Film Noir* (ed. E. Ann Kaplan, BFI Publishing, 1980), remain basic texts on their subject – like Laurie, the noir woman rather than the *femme fatale*.

ALSO PUBLISHED

· ·

If you would like further Information about future BFI Film Classics or about other books on film, media and popular culture from BFI Publishing, please write to:

**BFI Film Classics
British Film Institute
21 Stephen Street
London
W1P 2LN**

BFI Film Classics '... could scarcely be improved upon ... informative, intelligent, jargon-free companions.'
The Observer

Each book in the BFI Publishing Film Classics series honours a great film from the history of world cinema. With new titles published each year, the series is rapidly building into a collection representing some of the best writing on film. If you would like to receive further information about future Film Classics or about other books from BFI Publishing, please fill in your name and address and return this card to the BFI.*

No stamp is needed if posted in the UK, Channel Islands, or Isle of Man.

NAME

ADDRESS

POSTCODE

*North America: Please return your card to:
Indiana University Press, Attn: LPB, 601 N Morton Street,
Bloomington, IN 47401-3797

**BFI Publishing
21 Stephen Street
FREEPOST 7
LONDON
W1E 4AN**